Promise of the Soul

Promise of the Soul

Identifying and Healing Your Spiritual Agreements

DENNIS KENNY

John Wiley & Sons, Inc.

Published by John Wiley & Sons, Inc., New York
Published simultaneously in Canada

Design and production by Navta Associates, Inc.

The author gratefully acknowledges the permission of Laurie Garrett to include excerpts from her work in this book.

The author also gratefully acknowledges the permission of Angeles Arrien to use writings that appeared in a different form in her book, *The Four-Fold Way™: Walking the Paths of the Warrior, Teacher, Healer, and Visionary*, copyright © 1993 by Angeles Arrien; all rights reserved; San Francisco: HarperCollins, 1993. For further information about Arrien's work, please contact the office of Angeles Arrien, P.O. Box 2077, Sausalito, CA, 94966; www.angelesarrien.com.

This publication is designed to provide accurate and authoritative information in regard to the subject matter covered. It is sold with the understanding that the Publisher is not engaged in rendering professional services. If professional advice or other expert assistance is required, the services of a competent professional person should be sought.

Library of Congress Cataloging-in-Publication Data:

Kenny, Dennis
    Promise of the soul / Dennis Kenny.
        p. cm.
    Includes index.
    ISBN 0-471-41833-1 (alk. paper)
        1. Spiritual life. 2. Self-realization—Religious aspects. I. Title.
    BL624 .K46 2002
291.4'4—dc21   2001046861

Printed in the United States of America

10 9 8 7 6 5 4 3 2 1

To Eldora and Wilbert, my parents,
who gave me a great gift:
In my quiet moments
I always knew I was loved.

Contents

PART TWO
Balancing Your Promise

PART THREE
Changing Your Promise,
Changing Your Life

CONTENTS

Foreword

by Rachel Naomi Remen, M.D.

Some years ago, I attended a Yom Kippur service conducted by a very young Rabbi. Yom Kippur is the one of the most solemn and important of the Jewish Holy Days, a time of atonement for the sins of the past year in the hope of healing one's relationship with God. Having sat through many such services, I fully expected to hear the usual Yom Kippur sermon on the importance of repentance and forgiveness. But on his way to the podium, the rabbi reached out into the congregation and took his ten-month-old daughter from his wife. Carrying her in his arms, he stepped up to the podium and began his sermon.

At first the child stared wide-eyed at the large number of people before her, but after a few minutes, she reached out for her daddy's tie and put it into her mouth. Everyone smiled. Freeing his tie and tucking it back into his suit, the rabbi continued on with his sermon. But his tiny daughter, feeling his attention shift towards others, grabbed his glasses and pulled them off. People chuckled indulgently. Retrieving his glasses and settling them back in place, the rabbi kissed his child and went on with his sermon. A minute or so passed and then the little girl reached out and grabbed him by the nose. The entire congregation, including the rabbi, laughed aloud. Holding his daughter close and wrapping his prayer shawl around her, the rabbi waited. When the room again became still he asked his congregation, "Is there anything that she could do that you could not forgive her for?" People began to nod appreciatively, perhaps remembering their love for their own children and grandchildren. "And when does that end?" asked the rabbi. "At three? At fifteen? At thirty?" How old does someone have to be before you forget that everyone is a child of God?" There was an absolute silence. Very softly the rabbi asked, "And when did you forget that you too are a child of God?"

The rabbi's question speaks to a certain loneliness that is the hidden wound of our culture. It is also the question at the heart of this unique book. When did we forget that God loves us unconditionally? And how has forgetting the promise of God's love affected the way we live our lives?

Reverend Kenny suggests that even though we faithfully attend our churches and our synagogues, we meditate and we pray, many of us are living our lives in a constant struggle to become good enough to loved by God. Consciously or unconsciously, we operate from a fear-driven covenant with God and many of our behaviors and relationships are motivated by an effort to avoid God's judgment. When we become locked into an endless fearful striving to be someone other than who we are in order to deserve God's love, we have no place of refuge and safety. We have become homeless.

Perhaps this effort to avoid God's judgment causes much of the stress that characterizes our times. Stress is often thought to rooted in our unmet human needs, the result of a lack of personal intimacy and community, or an excess of time pressure and expectations. It is rarely thought of as a question of spirit. Yet Kenny suggests that the way we think about stress may be limited by the way we think of human nature. A sense of communion with God may be a fundamental human need. Perhaps a lack of communion is as stressful as a lack of community. Without feeling that we are held by God, we may become frightened and vulnerable, alone in the dark.

Certainly knowing that one is held by God can be enormously empowering for people in times of difficulty. In illness it may enable us to relinquish focus on a specific outcome, a fearfulness of the unknown, and find the courage to move forward. It may even help us to find peace in the face of uncertainty. Many years ago just before one of my own major surgeries, my surgeon leaned over the operating table and confided that there was a prayer he said before every surgery. Did I want him to say it aloud? When I nodded, he simply said "Dear God, help us to do here whatever is most right." I can still remember the power of these words. In an instant, they healed my fear and allowed me to meet the unknown with a deep sense of peace.

Perhaps knowing that we belong, that we are enough, may affect more than just our feelings of safety. A lack of communion may even affect our openness to being healed. After many years as a therapist to people with cancer, I am no longer surprised when someone tells me that, despite the many determined efforts they have made to find an effective treatment, at depth, they feel unworthy of becoming well again or unworthy of the concern and kindness of others around them. *Promise of the Soul* has made me wonder if what such people are really saying is that they are not good enough to be loved by God or to receive God's love through others. Perhaps we may need to heal our relationship with God in order to accept the gift of life?

Kenny cites several interesting studies that suggest that a sense of connection and belonging can affect not only the quality of life but survival itself. Community heals. Dr. David Speigel's research at Stanford demonstrated that connecting in a support group for a brief time every week for a year in the course of their illness can significantly lengthen survival for women with metastatic breast cancer. Dr. Dean Ornish's work suggests that an intense group support experience can help people reverse the sort of heart disease that otherwise requires surgical intervention. Increasingly, community seems to have a positive effect on survival. But who is to say that communion is not as important to survival and recovery as community? Soul loss, a loss of a sense of authentic connection with the source of life, was considered by the shamans and medicine men to be the root cause of all illness. Could a lack of authentic communion make us as vulnerable to illness as a lack of community?

In *Promise of the Soul*, Reverend Kenny raises these and many other challenging questions. But even more important, he has drawn together insights from his extensive professional practice as a counselor and his personal experience to enable us to better understand our covenants with God and to heal them. *Promise of the Soul* is a spiritual workbook. Through simple accessible exercises and reflections, Kenny offers us practical and proven methods that have enabled thousands of his counseling clients to relinquish their separation from God's love and live from the heart. It has been said that a human being is not a mechanism but an opportunity for the Infinite to manifest. Step by step, Kenny's approach shows us how we can release ourselves from self-imposed limitations and lifelong feelings of inadequacy to live a more soul-infused life. It is impossible to read this book without finding yourself somewhere in its pages and setting yourself free. It is a real opportunity.

Acknowledgments

This book would not have been written without the efforts of two people. First, Sarah Priestman, whose tireless enthusiasm, commitment, clarity, and partnership made this book happen. She has been a gift! Second, Gail Ross, my agent, whose belief in and commitment to this project were at times amazing. As she does her work, watching her walk a spiritual path has been a treat.

A special thank you to my editor, Tom Miller. His unerring eye and his invitation for me to be vulnerable have made this a better book.

Thank you to all of my students and clients who have been my teachers and have been willing to examine their covenants.

Lastly, thank you to Ruth Kenny for living with me while we each healed our covenants.

PART ONE

Identifying Your Promise

CHAPTER 1

The Promise of Your Soul

Why Healing Your Covenants Is Important

If you are disheartened or depressed, and you go to a medicine person or a shaman, they'll ask you one of four questions:

When in your life did you stop singing?

When in your life did you stop dancing?

When in your life did you stop being enchanted by stories,

Particularly your own life story?

—*Angeles Arrien, from* The Four-Fold Way™: Walking the Paths of the Warrior, Teacher, Healer, and Visionary

When did you stop singing? When did you stop dancing? These are important questions for any of us who follow a spiritual path, who seek to live in better health, or who simply want to live with less emotional turmoil and anxiety. These questions ask us to rediscover the joy and inspiration we once felt, to acknowledge the spirit and power that reside within. They point to the *promise of the soul*—the potential we all have to live in the fullest and most satisfying way we can possibly imagine. When we realize the promise of the soul, we find the creative impulse and deep wisdom that are always within us.

My work over the last 30 years has shown me that we can fulfill the promise of the soul when we create an authentic, loving relationship with God. You may wish to think of God as your Higher Power or your Creative Force; this is a personal choice. I use all these terms in this book.

We can actually co-create our lives with our Higher Power through the small moment-by-moment actions and choices that make up our day as well as through the big decisions we encounter that can loom large and feel overwhelming. At the foundation of this relationship is the covenant we have with God.

Our Spiritual Covenants

We all have a covenant with God, whether we know it or not. Our covenant is our unconscious promise to—our secret agreement with—our Higher Power that we usually make when we are children, although sometimes when we are adults. We develop prayers to God to maintain these covenants. Sometimes these covenants are healthy and lead to good things. All too often, though, our covenants are not healthy and can lead to problems and crises in our adult lives. If our covenants remain unexamined and unhealthy, we will keep on violating them, creating stress, unhappiness, and ill health.

The good news is that it is possible—in fact, it is important— to change and heal your childhood covenant. With this book, I hope to help you identify your covenant—your promise, your prayer—and help you change it so that you can heal.

I first began to explore the idea of covenants when I was a graduate student at the Andover-Newton Theological School in Newton Centre, Massachusetts, in the early seventies. We were asked to develop spiritual biographies as part of the psychology and pastoral counseling program, and though I had been involved in personal counseling work before, this required a deeper level of self-reflection than I had attempted in the past. I found myself articulating the covenant by which I tried to live my life and then defining what I believed would violate this covenant.

I had not realized it until I looked at my spiritual biography, but my covenant was based primarily on not hurting others. My unconscious prayer to God was that no one would be hurt or offended by my words or actions. Of course, this is impossible, and as I looked back over my life I found times when I did hurt people, even if I did not intend to. Everyone does.

As I thought about these instances, I realized that it felt less as if I had violated a prayer and more as if I had broken an agreement. And, as with breaking any agreement, I felt I had risked the anger of the one I'd made the promise to—in this case, God. These feelings perplexed me. How did my prayer evolve into an agreement? I let this question sift through my thoughts for months, finally realizing that the prayer was actually a tool I had developed to make good on an agreement I had made with God.

My Story

We all default to patterns that we learned as children, and these patterns often undermine the dreams we have for ourselves as adults. Our impulse to examine our childhoods is not necessarily an indication of whether our parents did a good job, nor is it only limited to those who came from severely dysfunctional homes. In fact, when we have the courage to step back and begin to clarify what works in our lives and what we want to change—

and then to take the personal responsibility to make those changes—it reflects positively on our upbringing.

In my case, I always felt my parents' love, but when I began to look at my life choices, I began to understand what I had learned as a child and how these lessons still influenced me as an adult. My father was a policeman in Detroit; my mother was a homemaker. My father's interest in law was based on values as much as order, so doing the right thing was a strong message. Since I was the son of a cop, word of my behavior always got back to him. I was a nice kid, but even stories of skirmishes on the playground or roughhousing on the ball field that can make up the fabric of an average boyhood day would make their way back to my house. Some kids feel as if they are being watched. In my case, I knew I was.

My mother was from a solid German Lutheran family; my father was Irish Catholic. I am sure she was the reason that church became a major part of our family's life as I was growing up. My mother was committed to my younger sister and me. Both of my parents worked hard to make it possible for us to have as many advantages as possible. My father was strong and held firmly to his values, and my mother was tough in her own right: She refused to show she was sick unless forced to. She was intense in her care and protection of her family.

My mother was the peacemaker. My father worked the night shift for many years, and she was vigilant about keeping the house quiet so that he could sleep during the day. Though he was most often even-tempered, he had the potential for anger. My mother worked hard to keep things running smoothly, as she did not want to give him a reason to react.

I learned that the way to be loved was to be peaceful and well behaved. I made a spiritual agreement to always be good. In the mind of a child, this guarantees love and recognition. That's why I prayed never to be the guy who hurts other people: On an unconscious level I believed that if I hurt someone, I would break my promise to God. Once I understood this reasoning, it was clear to me that I had lived for years with the fear of losing God's love because of the agreement I had made. I realized that we all carry secret agreements with God and live with the unconscious fear of breaking them.

I certainly brought these agreements into my marriage. My wife, Ruth, is an accomplished musician, conductor, and teacher who has produced and acted in community theater. We both entered marriage with strong needs to strive and be recognized. Our battles came as we sought to be acknowledged within our relationship in ways that would meet our needs. Ruth's ability to be spontaneous and direct with her feelings challenged my instinct to be in control and cautious. We have always been friends and our ability to have fun together has helped us bridge difficult times during our 30-year marriage.

Why I Wrote This Book

I am a hospital chaplain and the founding director of the Institute for Health and Healing, which is part of the California Pacific Medical Center, a large hospital in San Francisco. The institute is based on a multidisciplinary healing model, which allows me to combine my roles as an administrator, psychologist, and theologian. I am able to provide the major spiritual direction in our integrative medicine clinic.

For me, being able to participate consciously in the creation and ongoing efforts of the institute is a reflection of the healing work I have done over the years on my own covenant. I also credit healing my covenant with helping me to participate more fully in my marriage and strengthening my spiritual life. It has allowed me to recognize how the unconscious agreement I have with my Creative Force can undermine my own power, taking me down a road that ultimately does not serve my purpose or fulfill my dream. When I am aware of this, I bring the lessons of my healed covenant into my daily decisions and interactions. I am then able to connect with the promise of my soul.

I wrote this book because I want to share the possibility of this experience with others. In addition to my own healing, I have seen the impact of covenants on hundreds of patients and students over the past 30 years. I have witnessed over and over the insights and changes that result when people are able to identify their secret agreement with God. I have worked with individuals as they begin to understand the impact of this unconscious promise. Once they do, they can work to heal the agreement to create a more cooperative, inclusive relationship with their Higher Power.

Promise of the Soul will help you realize that the agreement you made with God years ago may no longer serve you. Once you accept this realization, you can begin to explore creating a relationship with your Higher Power that will strengthen you spiritually and, in turn, empower you to live a healthier life.

The Two Kinds of Covenants

In divinity school, after I realized we all have secret covenants we carry with us, I studied the use of the words *promise* and *covenant* in the Bible. This led me to the discovery that there are actually two kinds of covenants: one that comes from on high, as if it is the final authority, and one that is developed more in the spirit of co-creation. The first is described by the promise made by God to Abraham when He gave him "many children," all of whom were to live under His law.

"As long as you follow My law," He told Abraham, "I will be your God and you will be my people."

There are myriad interpretations of God's promise to Abraham, all of which hold valuable teachings. For the sake of relating the story to healing our personal covenants with God, however, the most important recognition is that it was a law that came from on high.

In the age of Abraham, this kind of edict was exactly what was needed to help create the systems and structures that were required. Additional laws that grew out of this covenant were later sent to Moses in the form of the Ten Commandments. For most of us, the image of Moses accepting the Ten Commandments—written on stone tablets and delivered to him from a dark sky, high atop a mountain—is deeply ingrained in our consciousness. It is the image of the unquestionable law.

This is the same power we unconsciously give to our own covenant—as if it were unquestionable and out of our hands. As I discovered, however, and as you will learn as you read this book, your covenant may feel as if it has the authority of God, but you are really the only one who can give it power.

The focus of the second type of covenant can seen be in Hebrews 9.11:

> The days are surely coming,
> says the Lord,
> when I will establish a new covenant . . .
> not like the covenant that I made with their
>   ancestors,
> for they did not continue in my covenant,
> I will put my laws in their minds,
> And write them on their hearts,
> And I will be their God,
> And they shall be my people.
> And they shall not teach one another
> Or say to each other, "Know the Lord,"
> For they shall all know me,
> From the least of them to the greatest,
> And I will remember their sins no more.

This covenant does not ask for obedience. Instead, God trusts that "I will be their God, and they shall be my people." When Jesus was questioned about healing the sick on the Sabbath, He explained that it was more important to offer help to the needy than to obey the law. Because stories in the Bible are often used to illustrate a point, many people believe that this shows the new covenant allows for a co-created, empowered relationship rather than a promise that must never be questioned.

At this point in my life, while in divinity school, I had been working as a spiritual counselor long enough to see that people yearned for meaning and purpose. I also knew that no matter how deep our faith, we need to take responsibility for our actions in order to grow. As I understood it, the lesson of this covenant was personal responsibility.

Personal Responsibility: The Faith-Based Covenant

We can re-create our original, unquestionable, *law-based covenant* to reflect the spirit of a more flexible, empowered covenant. We do not necessarily have to toss out the old promise and establish a new one. Instead, we can choose to keep what works about our promise and add what we need in order to create balance. It's a matter of shifting the way we state the agreement so that we move out of a conditional, law-based promise and into a *faith-based covenant*.

A law-based, *conditional* covenant usually resembles this statement: "As long as I am doing for others, then I know my Higher Power will take care of me." It is an agreement that promises us God's love, approval, or acceptance—it is different for each of us—in exchange for behaving in a way that is good, productive, or imaginative—again, it depends on who we are and what our original covenant was.

Faith-based covenants, however, allow us to live in a more cooperative, unconditional relationship with God. With a faith-based covenant, we never risk losing God's love or acceptance, as we know it is always there. Instead, our promises—and our willingness to be mindful of them—affect our relationship with God. For example, if your law-based covenant is, "When I am strong, God will love me," your faith-based covenant might be, "When I am open to my softness as well as to my strength, I deepen my relationship with God." Again, feel free to substitute Higher Power, Creative Force, or whatever works for you in place of God, if you choose.

It is important to understand that the wording of your faith-based covenant is not about winning or losing with God. Instead, it automatically puts you in an authentic relationship with your Higher Power. And living as your most mindful and authentic self, you will deepen this connection. Your faith-based covenant is based on the understanding that you can co-create your life with God.

If you re-create your covenants, you will find your relationship with God or your Higher Power to be less judgmental and more empowering. You can live as if God is within you rather than above you. You will know that though you have God's love, your actions are not in anyone's hands but your own. Living with your faith-based covenant means that it will be up to you to choose when you are ready to live in the glory of God, in the light of universal love, or with mindful, enlightened compassion—however spirituality is most authentic for you.

Spirituality: Our Relationship with God

Because I am inviting you to consider the possibility that healing your covenants can have an impact on your spirituality, I want to let you know what I mean when I refer to spirituality. I will begin by describing my own understanding of God and then move into the meaning of spirituality in the context of healing covenants.

For me, God or the Higher Power is best described as a Creative Force. The Creative Force is at the base of who we are individually and grounds us in our very being. It brought us into existence, and it gives our lives meaning. I can access my Creative Force either by traveling inside to hear its interior voice, or by reaching outside and seeing its wonder and truth reflected in our world.

I have also had the experience of the Creative Force reaching into me to touch my inner world, bringing me clarity and peace. I might experience the Creative Force intensely in times of glory or prayer. I experience the Creative Force through an ongoing, mindful awareness of the complexity and grace I see around me.

St. Augustine, a philosopher and theologian of early Christianity who lived from A.D. 354 to 430, wrote some beautiful lines that express my experience of the Creative Force. His words are ancient, but their meaning rings fresh and true:

> But what do I love when I love my God? Not material beauty of a temporal nature; nor the brilliance of earthly light, so welcome to our eyes; not the fragrance of flowers, perfumes and spices; not manna or honey; not limbs such as the body delights to embrace. It is not these that I love when I love my God. And yet . . . it is true that I love a light of a certain kind, a voice, a perfume, a food, an embrace; but they are of the kind that I love in my inner self, when my soul is bathed in light that is not bound by space; when it listens to sound that never dies away; when it breathes fragrance that is not borne away on the wind; when it tastes food that is never consumed by eating; when it clings to an embrace from which it is not severed by fulfillment of desire. That is what I love when I love my God.

In terms of healing our covenants, spirituality is the way in which our relationship with God, the Higher Power, or the Creative Force comes to life. When we are in sync with our agreement with God, our connection to the sacred is a natural part of our day. It is the truest realization of the promise of the soul.

If we are unsure about our agreement with God, we risk living with a sense of spirituality that is confused, hypocritical, or empty. When we are not in touch with our agreements in any relationship, we cannot participate fully. When the relationship is with God, our unconscious agreements keep us from experiencing our spirituality in all its grace and power.

When we heal our covenants and create a new agreement with God or our Higher Power, we deepen our relationship with every choice we make.

What Is Your Covenant Style?

Identifying your covenant is the first step toward healing it. But how do you know where to start? If your covenant is unconscious, how do you determine what it is and how it influences your life? This book guides you through a step-by-step process that will help you to recognize and heal your covenant.

We start with an exploration of how we create covenants, exploring their impact on both spirituality and health. We will then begin the journey of identifying our own covenants.

Most of us tend toward three different covenant styles, which I call *Givers*, *Wanters*, and *Searchers*. We all have aspects of each of them in our lives, of course, but in order to hone in on our covenant we need to understand which of these styles dominates our choices and our lives. I have developed a Covenant Styles Questionnaire to help you clarify which of the styles is most pervasive in your life. Though you may find that you identify with one style in one set of circumstances—at home, for example—

Covenant Styles Questionnaire

Please check the description in each line that best fits you.

God (my Higher Power) is
☐ watching   ☐ responsible   ☐ exciting

My parents' love was
☐ demanding   ☐ distant   ☐ inconsistent

In my life, I must
☐ connect   ☐ succeed   ☐ search

My strongest desire in life is to
☐ contribute   ☐ accomplish   ☐ discover

In crises I blame
☐ myself   ☐ others   ☐ no one

When I feel stress, I
☐ help   ☐ get irritated   ☐ flee

I feel I am
☐ friendly   ☐ intense   ☐ interesting

I talk about
☐ people/feelings   ☐ goals   ☐ adventure

In decisions I
☐ seek consensus   ☐ stay on the path   ☐ consider all options

I avoid
☐ standing up for myself   ☐ being vulnerable   ☐ making commitments

The purpose of love is to
☐ serve   ☐ receive   ☐ discover

and another style in other situations, the key is to identify the style that most heavily determines your choices. It will become the beacon that lights the way toward your covenant, as it is more than a simple personality choice: Your style is the behavior you have developed in order to keep your unconscious agreement with God.

How to score the questionnaire: The first column reveals traits of the Giver; the second column reflects those of the Wanter; the third, of the Searcher. Take a look at the column in which you have checked the most boxes—this will let you know which model is the one you tend to default to the most. Now take a look at the column with the least amount of checks. This style is the one that you do not have access to right now, but have the potential to include in your life. The remaining column represents the style that you have learned to use as adaptive behavior, but you may not feel it is a true part of you.

While knowing your dominant style is imperative to identifying your covenant, understanding the roles that all three styles play is the key to creating balance. This understanding will help you discover why you learned to stop singing, why you learned to stop dancing. You can then choose to integrate these parts of yourself back into your life.

Your Promise Breaker

As you explore the style you developed in order to keep your promise with God, you will also confront the behavior choices I call *Promise Breakers*. Promise Breakers are the things we believe we can never do. They are seemingly benign behaviors that we observe in other people all the time—the ability to speak up for yourself, for example, or to take risks in intimate relationships— but that have always been a challenge for us. In many cases, we have cut ourselves off so successfully from our Promise Breakers that we do not know they are available to us.

The truth is that our Promise Breakers are the very things we need to integrate into our lives in order to live in balance and health.

When we live with faith-based covenants, our choices are in alignment with the promise of the soul. Healing our covenants involves understanding our agreement with God, creating a new relationship with our Higher Power, and integrating all parts of ourselves to live in balance. It is through co-creating our lives with God that we can realize a life filled with truth, health, happiness, wisdom, and love.

CHAPTER 2

God and Your Spirituality

Grace strikes us when we are in great pain and restlessness. It strikes us when we walk through the dark valley of a meaningless and empty life. It strikes us when our disgust for our own being, our indifference, our weakness, our hostility, and our lack of direction and composure have become intolerable to us. . . . Sometimes at that moment a wave of light breaks into our darkness, and it is as though a voice were saying, "You are accepted."

—*Paul Tillich from* Prayers for Healing

One truth, many doors.

—*Swami Satchidananda*

Second Chances: Charles's Story

I received a phone call in the middle of the night several years ago from one of my patients, Charles (all of the names in this book have been changed, as have any identifying circumstances). It is not uncommon for people to contact me at home, or at night, but this call was a surprise, as I had not heard from Charles for a while. He was calling from his hospital bed, as he had just been admitted for his second heart attack. I hurried to see him. I first met Charles two years before this call under similar circumstances—his initial heart attack—so I knew this was serious.

Before he first called, Charles and I already knew each other casually through a professional connection. He explained that he was contacting me after talking to his therapist and his closest friend about the heart attack, but now he wanted to understand what was happening in his life "from a spiritual point of view."

Charles told me that he had driven himself to the emergency room and waited for two hours before being admitted, explaining that he did not want to "bother" the staff. I wondered why it was easier for Charles to sit quietly than it was for him to ask for what he needed, even when his heart was failing. His cardiologist was keeping him for observation, so we had a chance to meet several times, and it became clear that his decision not to draw attention to himself was a pattern in his life. His marriage had also been a place in which he chose to sit quietly, despite the pain he felt. He described his wife as an alcoholic, but said she refused treatment. He was afraid for her and upset about the marriage, as he could see her health declining and their relationship deteriorating, but he would not take steps to change the situation. He felt he had to stand by her no matter how she behaved.

Charles was in his mid-40s. He told me that he wanted to reach 50. When he asked me what I thought was at the root of the attack, I told him it might be his inability to see that he was sacrificing himself to his idea of commitment. I thought his heart was sick, I said, and he needed to take care of it on an emotional level. I told him he needed to stand up for himself in order to heal.

"Okay, thanks," he'd answered flatly, as if we were discussing a benign subject that had nothing to do with life and death. "But I don't think that's it. Thanks, anyway."

When I walked into Charles's room two years later, he greeted me warmly. He told me that the intervening time had been difficult. His wife's drinking had escalated, she had lost her job, and their lives were in chaos. Then he let me know that his doctors warned him that this attack was so serious that he might not be able to work again.

"I think you might have been on to something when we talked the first time," he said. "So what do we do now?"

We chatted briefly that night and met for many sessions afterward, exploring how his commitment to others sabotaged his own life—in this case, his very survival. We looked at how he could still nurture others—which, when done consciously, could be a way for Charles to strengthen his heart—but also empower himself. There was no reason for Charles to stop caring for others; he just needed to balance it with his own needs.

As we worked together, we uncovered the covenant that Charles had made with God. It was a conditional covenant: He felt he would receive God's love as long as he was a good and caring person. According to Charles, keeping his commitments was the ultimate way to be this caring, giving person. If he confronted his wife about her disease, he explained to me, it would be a challenge to his commitment. In his eyes, it would appear that he didn't really care, and if that happened, he believed he would lose God's love.

Charles knew he needed to change. He had the evidence of what happened when he lived with the conditional covenant: It literally broke his heart. I did not ask Charles to turn his back on the idea of commitment. Instead, I guided him to change his current covenant in two ways: first, to include supporting himself in his commitment to care for others, and second, to do so without making God's love contingent on his behavior.

His new covenant may at first seem to be a simple tweak of language, but in reality it offers a complex shift in meaning. *As long as I am committed to myself as I am to others,* Charles now believes, *I will be more fully present in my relationship with God.*

This covenant allows Charles to balance his own needs with those of others. Once he was able to do this, he found he could truly pursue his dream of a caring, supportive relationship, as now he is able to take his own needs as seriously as those of others. When he looked at his marriage in terms of his new covenant, he recognized that unless his wife sought treatment, his needs would not be met. He left the marriage, making a strong internal commitment to find balance in his next relationship.

Charles has kept in touch with me over the years. He sends cards from the vacations he takes with his new wife, who he said makes him happier than he ever knew he could be. He also sent me a postcard when he turned 50. It was a drawing of a deep red heart, with a message from Charles written across it in big bold letters: "I'm here!"

Even if you dispute the existence of God, you have made deals with life itself, or agreements about the way things are supposed to be. Covenants are not always something that you need to reject or fix, but they are the kind of idea that is so much a part of your perspective that you rarely question whether you can step back and reconsider them. And in this blind acceptance, you surrender your ability to choose.

Unbeknownst to you, these covenants—or promises—are conditional: *If I work hard, I will be taken care of. If I tend to those in need, I will be loved. If I am kind, God will protect me.* It is critical to understand your covenants, especially if you are on a path to imbue your life with more meaning or to increase your experience of spirituality. If you are one of many who have pursued a deeper purpose in life but keep coming up feeling as if you are somehow missing the mark or falling short, the reason may be embedded within your conditional law-based covenant.

Have You Already Resolved Your Issues?

Even if you have done a lot of psychological work on yourself, resolving the many issues that get ferried from childhood into adulthood, your covenant may still dominate your behaviors, especially in the face of stress. In times of crisis, illness, or even great fortune—anytime you need to respond with flexibility and balance—you may default to a part of yourself you thought you had remedied years ago.

This is also true for those of us on a spiritual journey. We may find new teachings in other traditions, and we may be drawn to them more than to the ones with which we were raised. We might discover spiritual practices that bring us closer to God than those we knew as children. We might get down from the pew and onto the meditation cushion. We might hear the voice of our creator in the silence of nature, or maybe we sing God's praises, shaking the rafters of our newfound church with an energy that would have been shameful in the church in which we grew up. We might use new language when we describe our spiritual paths, replacing commandments, scripture, and sin with compassion, mindfulness, and grace.

And then a crisis hits. For most of us, the fellowship and practice of our new path offers great support in crisis. But you may also find yourself plummeting back to a belief in God that you thought you had left long ago. You may have learned about self-forgiveness on your new path, but in the face of crisis you blame yourself unmercifully. You may have embraced the teaching of compassion, but in stress you find yourself lashing out at others, as if what you are going through was their doing. Or you may find you have committed to a practice that keeps you grounded and focused, but then you find yourself floundering just when you need support the most.

This situation raises some profound questions.

- If there is a chance you might turn to God in times of need, wouldn't it be wise to turn to a God whose teachings reflect your life now?

- If faith really has a role in healing, shouldn't you examine your spiritual beliefs?

- Is it possible you are living your life according to spiritual agreements you are not aware of?

- If so, can they sustain you in times of need?

- How do you know when your spiritual beliefs help you realize the promise of your soul?

The Gift of the Promise Breaker

When I first began to introduce the idea of covenants into my counseling practice, I came up against a challenge. My clients were compelled by the idea of looking at their secret agreements with God, and the concept of law-based versus faith-based covenants resonated with almost everyone. I needed a way for people to identify their old covenant so that they could move on to developing a new one.

One afternoon I was using the idea of covenants in a training exercise for a spiritual counseling class. The students were sharing their covenants with each other, identifying the promise they had made to God and how it influenced their lives. One of the students stood up and told the class that at a young age he remembered being struck by the passage "The meek shall inherit the Earth." He had promised God that he would always be meek and would always care for others who seemed poor or helpless. As he was explaining how this felt, he looked around the room as if to make sure that his classmates understood him. He was not satisfied with this promise anymore, he told us. He wanted to be more powerful, but he just could not imagine it.

"If I was strong," he said, "it feels as if I would be breaking a promise. It feels like it would be unforgivable. That's what keeps me from being strong."

Another classmate rose to her feet and spoke directly to him. "It feels to me like I would be breaking a promise if I was meek," she said. "I always have to be strong. Maybe I could use some of your covenant to balance me. You could certainly use some of mine. Maybe we could share."

I realized that it was not just the covenant that people needed to identify; it was also the very thing that would violate it—that is, the *Promise Breaker*. And they did not just need to identify it; they also needed to integrate it into their lives. My student was on the right track when she asked to share her colleague's covenant—but she did not need to use his. She had the ability to tap into her own meekness. As her Promise Breaker, it was the part of her that she had cut off from her awareness, and this was limiting her chances for wholeness and balance.

Breaking Your Promise to Heal Your Life

Healing covenants requires you to look deep inside and to face parts of yourself you have turned your back on for years. But you cannot only look at these parts of yourself. You must also be willing to include them in your everyday life, even if they are the kinds of things that you once promised God you would never consider.

I am not talking about destructive behaviors, of course, but those that you have determined are not within your reach or are not safe to call your own. You may discover empowerment, vulnerability, and focus to be virtues. Possibly since childhood, whether you know it or not, many of you have promised God that you would not be as powerful as you could be. Or you have made an agreement with your Higher Power that you would not reveal your neediness. You have learned to deny these elements of yourself. When you change your covenants, you choose to honor these parts.

This means taking responsibility for your beliefs, your attitudes, and your actions in a whole new way. It means looking at the parts of yourself that you consider negative or forbidden, which is something even those of us who devote a lot of time and energy to self-understanding do not always do. Even if you are on an ongoing journey of personal growth and feel that you are comfortable with your inner world, you will most likely touch upon new, unresolved areas when you begin to understand the secret agreements you have made with God.

Think about how you feel when you break an agreement, whether it is showing up late to a scheduled meeting or breaking a vow you've made to someone you love. Most people do their best to keep agreements and feel deep regret when they are broken. Now imagine breaking a promise you made with God. For many, just the thought stops them in their tracks. If you even consider doing something that you think might challenge your spiritual agreement, it can feel as if you have betrayed both the highest power you know of and the deepest part of yourself.

Most of the Promise Breakers that people describe are totally acceptable behaviors—unless, of course, your conditional agreement with God dictates otherwise. They are common, everyday choices that you are so hardwired to avoid, because of your law-based covenants, that it would never occur to you to choose them. Your Promise Breaker might be that you will never do the following:

- Trust other people
- Expose your feelings
- Speak up for yourself
- Ask for help
- Appear dependent
- Give up freedom
- Accept praise
- Tolerate boredom
- Be penned in
- Tell others what to do
- Take orders
- Accept help
- Admit fault

This list points to the innocuous nature of the Promise Breaker. Behaviors that appear appropriate to others can feel like the actions you must avoid at all costs, depending on your covenants. But they are also the very behaviors you need to accept, because by excluding them you keep yourself focused on maintaining a conditional agreement. You also create tension and imbalance when you keep these parts of yourself in denial.

Most of us spend a lot of valuable energy keeping our Promise Breakers under wraps. I will explore the impact of these secrets on our health in later chapters.

Creating the Faith-Based Covenant

Creating a new covenant is not a matter of tossing out an old promise and establishing a new one. When you change your covenant, you keep what works about your agreement and add what you need from your Promise Breaker in order to create balance. The real difference is not in what you agree to do, but in the way you state it. When you heal your covenants, you move out of a conditional law-based covenant into a faith-based one.

The faith-based covenant is rooted in the idea that you co-create your life with God. I heard Dr. John Kinney, Dean at the Samuel D. Proctor School of Theology, Richmond, Virginia, address this idea by taking issue with the common phrase "one nation under God." As a minister, he saw many people who, in social terms, were always thought of as being "under." Some felt they were under the oppression of racism or class; others felt underrepresented or undermined. They were not under anything, Dr. Kinney argued, and he did not think their language should reflect this negative assumption. For him, the way the phrase rang true was to say "one nation *with* God."

I agree with his point. With a simple turn of a phrase he shifts the power from coming from above to being alongside, in cooperation. This is the spirit of the faith-based covenant. The promise is made with a God who is not only almighty, but also beside us and within us. This is a way of thinking about God that shifts the responsibility from Creator to Co-creator. When we get ourselves out from under the divine and work with God, we are taking responsibility for our lives.

The same power that some of us project onto God is given by others to the process of meditation, or to ritual, or to any symbol or practice that renders us devout. But in reality, authentic inner change is made by us, in concert with spiritual practice or our ideas about God.

When you live with your new covenant, your life is not in God's hands. God can be as omnipresent as you would like, but you are still responsible for your own life. This does not mean you are not grateful for blessings. It does not mean your prayers are for naught. It does not minimize your experiences of divin-

26

ity or grace, and it does not ask you to question your faith, no matter what your calling.

All it means is that God is within you and alongside of you. It means that when you are ready to live in the glory of God, in the light of universal love, or with mindful, enlightened compassion—however spirit is most authentic for you—it is up to you to choose.

Covenants and Your Spirituality: The Many Definitions of God

In my line of work, I constantly come across brochures and magazine articles using the words *spirit, spirituality, God, faith, Higher Power, grace, divinity, peace.* After a while, these terms can begin to run together.

Sometimes I feel as if the many terms used to describe the experience of God or spirit have become like the dots in an impressionist painting. When you stand back from the canvas you can see an image—water lilies, or the Cathedral of Notre Dame—but if you move in a little closer, you can easily tell that the picture is really an accumulation of separate dabs of color. Up close, you recognize how the image changed each time the artist's brush touched the canvas. You can see that every brush stroke is different, and each has made its own contribution. When you step back again, these distinctions are lost—but the beauty of the art remains.

The many ways in which we talk about God add up to create the beauty of our faith, but unless we step in for a closer look we lose track of how each one makes a critical difference. When we work with our covenants, we need to look at the details that add up to the big picture—because, in this case, the canvas is where we create our lives.

What Is Your Definition of God?

If we are going to examine the agreement that is at the root of our spiritual experience, we need to look at how we approach spirituality in the first place. For me, as I mentioned in the first chapter, God is the Creative Force that resides at the core of who we each are. I experience my connection to this force in stillness and action and in solitude and community, as my connection is based more on my awareness of being in tune with God than setting aside a time and place for worship, though this is important as well. For me, devotion is a matter of recognizing the grace and power that are the gifts of being alive. When I am mindful of the mysterious unity of life and the generous energy of the Creative Force, I am in touch with what many people call God.

But mine is just one way to experience the divine. For some people, God exists outside of them—perhaps in Heaven, keeping a watchful eye. This God may be protective, judgmental, inclusive, forgiving, or benign. For others, there is a feeling of the divine spirit that resides within them, and this is where they go to experience their faith. This may require solitude and silence, or it may be invoked through community, arts, or nature. And God may also be both within and outside of the self—it all depends on individual beliefs.

Some say their God delivers salvation or an afterlife. Others believe in reincarnation, or that the karma we create in one lifetime follows us into another. Joan Borysenko talks about this variety of spiritual experiences in *The Ways of the Mystic*:

> Different religions and paths to God suit different personality types. Some of us relate to God best through the intellect, others through the emotions. Some crave ritual; others thrive on simplicity. Hasidic Jews and Sufi (Islamic) dervishes relate to God as the Beloved, and enter the state of unity through joyful singing and dance. Native Ameri-

cans and other First Nations People find God through nature and community, prayer and ceremony. Christians, who comprise five hundred diverse sects, may find God through intellect, ritual, song, service, grace, prayer, or the transubstantiation of bread and wine into the body and blood of Jesus. Buddhists find enlightenment through discipline of the mind, the precepts of right living, meditation, prayer, and the practice of compassion.

EXERCISE 1

What Do You Believe?

I understand that my rendering of a Creative Force is just one way of looking at God. This exercise provides a good opportunity for you to step back and take a look at how you approach your Higher Power and spirituality. I realize, of course, that some of you may not be willing to open this up for discussion. The following questions simply allow you to deepen your understanding of your own beliefs. This understanding not only helps with covenants, but will ultimately strengthen your connection to your own path. Use a journal and write down your answers, allowing yourself the time you need for your deepest thoughts to surface.

Ask yourself about your own Higher Power.

1. Does it exist in all things or does it exist separately?

2. Have you been touched by the Spirit, God, or a Higher Power? How? Did the experience come from outside or within?

3. Does your Higher Power forgive you, judge you, or do both?

4. Do you believe you have been here before?

5. Do you believe you will exist in some form after this life?

Read over your answers from start to finish before moving on. Does anything surprise you? Do you have any feelings or discomfort? If so, you might want to take a few more minutes to reflect on these feelings. Turn to a new page in your journal and allow yourself to explore how you feel when you look at your definition of the Higher Power.

Once you are clear about how you understand your Higher Power, the next step is to look at your spirituality. I often hear people talking about God and spirituality as if they are interchangeable. They are related, but they are not the same. It is important to clarify them as we look at our covenants.

Spirituality Is a Reflection

Spirituality is a reflection of your relationship with God, your Higher Power, or your Creative Force. This reflection is expressed through your practice. I work with the idea of spirituality as a personal agreement with God, a Creative Force, or a guiding power that is sustainable in the face of investigation, crisis, and prosperity.

Your spirituality is sustainable when your agreement with God nurtures and guides you no matter what happens in your life, whether you are faced with tragedy or touched by luck. It is the deepest way of fulfilling the promise of your soul. Spirituality is a natural part of your everyday existence, not just something that gets revved up when you need an extra jolt of universal energy to get you through the latest crisis. When you are at peace with your agreements with God, your experience of the sacred flows in and out of your day.

This is the cornerstone of spirituality—that it is with us, always.

Ask Yourself About Your Spirituality

All relationships are strengthened when we understand what we bring to them, what we expect from them, and what we need to become more sensitive to them. If our spirituality is a reflection of our relationship to God, it needs our care and understanding. Take out your journal again and explore your spirituality and relationship to God.

1. How does your spiritual life fulfill the promise of your soul?

2. Do you experience love from your Higher Power?

3. What do you depend on in your relationship with God?

4. What do you not expect to experience in this relationship?

5. What is the nature of your worship or practice?

6. Is your practice done in community or in isolation?

7. Is your practice focused on service or on introspection and understanding?

8. What does it feel like when you are reflecting your belief in God?

9. What does it feel like when your actions do not reflect your spiritual beliefs?

10. Do you have a vision for your spiritual life? Where are you heading?

Take a few minutes to review your answers. If you feel that you missed something or are taken in by something you have written, give yourself the time you need to delve a little deeper. You will become increasingly aware of your relationship to God as you heal your covenants, so whatever you are beginning to get in touch with as you finish this exercise will support you in your process.

EXERCISE 3

Write to Your Higher Power

Here's an exercise that may help you to deepen your understanding of the relationship you have with God.

1. Imagine that your Higher Power asks you a question.

2. Take an imaginative leap and answer the question as if you were writing a letter.

3. Address it to whatever force helps you to chart the course of higher meaning in your life, as if you were writing to someone you know—because, really, isn't this someone you know?

4. Describe the promise of your soul. Talk about what you know is possible in your life. Reveal your biggest dreams.

5. Once you have described your dreams, explore how your relationship with God or your Higher Power can help you realize this vision.

6. Tell God or your Higher Power what you appreciate in the relationship, and let your Higher Power know what you bring to the dynamic that you feel good about.

7. Then take the risk to tell God or your Higher Power what you wish were different.

8. If you are looking for something to change, take another risk. State in the letter what you are willing to change in

yourself as well as what you want to see change in your Higher Power.

9. When you are done with the letter, notice how you signed off.

Your Life Prayer

Your life prayer is the first thought that surfaces in your soul when you wake up in the morning. It may not be something you are conscious of, but it flows through your thoughts throughout the day, informing all of your decisions, responses, and dreams. Some prayers are based on specific ideas or outcomes: turning to a Higher Power for help, thanking God, confessing your sins, asking for forgiveness. The life prayer is less intentional. It resides in your unconscious as a core message about how you believe you need to live each day. Examples of the life prayer are "I must be strong," or "Others need me."

Your prayer was developed in order to keep your covenant. Every time you say your life prayer, you solidify your spiritual agreement. If you pray to be strong, you may have a conditional agreement that bases God's love on your ability to persevere through the toughest times. If you wake up with the feeling that you better get up and start the day because so many people are counting on you, you may discover a spiritual agreement that binds you to serving others, sometimes at the expense of your own well-being.

Since the life prayer is often just the thought you wake up with, you may greet the light of morning asking God to help you just get through another day, or you may open your eyes and immediately hone in on your "to do" list. Maybe you ruminate on solving the problems you anticipate will fill your day; maybe you try to figure out how to avoid them.

You may already be deciding, "Well, this certainly has nothing to do with me. I just lie under the covers and think about my toast and coffee." Or you may be shaking your head and saying, "Like I have time for this in the morning? I jump out of bed and start making sandwiches for all the lunchboxes."

If so, what would your prayer or intention be if you had one? If one doesn't come to mind, use the following exercise to write about what you imagine it would be. It is *your* journal and *your* blank page, so allow yourself the time to dig down inside. You might want to just start by writing, "When I wake up in the morning, my prayer, or my intention, is to . . . ," and as you fill in the rest, your prayer may very well emerge.

EXERCISE 4

Exercise Your Life Prayer

1. What is your prayer?

2. Does it reflect what you know is possible for your life?

3. If you could make up a prayer to help you fulfill the promise of your soul, what would you say?

4. If you could make up a prayer that thanked God for all your fortune, what would you say?

5. If your prayer requested guidance to help you live in a more conscious way, what would you ask for?

6. If you wanted to assure God that you were living a good life, what parts of your life would you include? What would you leave out?

When you create a faith-based covenant, your life prayer changes. You learn to base your prayer on deepening your relationship with God through your actions. Instead of limiting your choices to the conditions of an old covenant, your life prayer now helps to guide you on the path that leads to the promise of your soul. Instead of asking for God to help in your effort to support others, for example, you may pray to speak up for your own needs as you express your generous spirit. Or if you have always prayed to be strong, your faith-based life prayer may ask God to help you see the power of your hidden softness.

We will return to this life prayer when we find our new covenant, creating for ourselves the prayer that inspires our empowered agreement with God every day.

In the book *Eternal Echoes*, John O'Donohue asks us to create a prayer that is "worthy of the destiny" to which we have been called:

> Listen to the voices of longing in your soul. Listen to your hungers. Give attention to the unexpected that lives around the rim of your life. Listen to your memory and to the onrush of your future, to the voices of those near you and those you have lost. Out of all that, make a prayer that is big enough for your wild soul, yet tender enough for your shy and awkward vulnerability; that has enough healing to gain the ointment of divine forgiveness for your wounds; enough truth and vigor to challenge your blindness and complacency; enough graciousness and vision to mirror your immortal beauty. Write a prayer that is worthy of the destiny to which you have been called.

Is your prayer big enough for your wild soul? As you understand your old agreement, your prayers can embrace the truth and vigor, the graciousness and vision of your new covenant.

Our Covenants, Our Choices

There are many ways to understand God. And since our spirituality reflects our relationship with God, there are endless ways in which this comes to life. In *A Path with Heart,* Jack Kornfield tells us how to begin:

> We discover that no one can define for us exactly what our path should be. Instead, we must allow the mystery and beauty of this question to resonate within our being. Then somewhere within us an answer will come and understanding will arise. If we are still and listen deeply, even for a moment, we will know if we are following a path with heart.

As we explore our covenants, the important thing to remember is that no matter what our ideas are about God and no matter how we live out our spirituality, our covenants come from within us. When we live with agreements that we create from our most loving, conscious selves, we follow a path with heart to the promise of our souls.

CHAPTER 3

Healing Covenants

Mind, Body, and Spirit

The greatest revolution of our generation is the discovery
that human beings, by changing the inner attitudes of
their minds, can change the outer aspects of their lives.

—*William James*

There is an ancient Buddhist story that tells of a grieving mother
who carried the body of her deceased young daughter from town
to town begging for help, as if she could still save her. She was
turned away again and again, as everyone could see there was no
hope for the child. Finally, someone told her that the Buddha
could help.

The mother journeyed to the Buddha and begged him to
save her child.

"I can help you," he said, "but you must first go and find a mustard seed and bring it back to me."

The mother was overjoyed, as she knew she could do this.

"I will go right away," she said, and, holding the body of her child against her, she prepared to go.

The Buddha stopped her as she began to leave. "One more thing," he said. "You must bring the seed from a home that has not experienced death."

As the woman knocked on doors to find a home that had been spared death, she encountered the sorrow and empathy of others. She heard their stories and felt their compassion, and was eventually able to put her child to rest and accept her loss.

In this story, the cure the woman is seeking—to bring her child back to life—is not possible. The only thing that can heal her pain is her own acceptance. The pain does not exist on a physical level, and the Buddha recognized this. He did not tell her to rest, to try a certain cure, or to put down the heavy body of her child. The illness was not designated to her body; nor was it just in her spirit or her mind. The despair took hold of her whole being. He knew that by accepting her loss she would heal on a whole level, which is why he directed her to others who had also grieved.

There are similar parables of healing in Christianity. When people approached Jesus to be healed, He asked them about their journey, their family, or their faith. When Jesus healed the sick, He often did so not by reducing the pain in their bodies, but by listening and guiding them to understand what they were seeking emotionally and spiritually.

One story describes a meeting between Jesus and a blind man begging by the roadside. When the blind man heard that Jesus of Nazareth was about to pass, he cried, "Jesus, Son of David, have mercy on me!"

Those who were in front of Jesus rebuked the man, telling him to be quiet, but he cried out even more. When Jesus reached him,

He stopped and asked the man, "What do you want me to do for you?"

"Let me receive my sight, Oh Lord," he answered.

"Receive your sight," Jesus told the man. "Your faith has made you well."

These stories illustrate the philosophy of the mind–body–spirit medical model. When someone is in need of healing, the whole being must be treated. A patient's lifestyle, attitude, spirituality, and psychological issues are weighed with comparable emphasis on symptoms, lab tests, and family history. The model promotes wellness as much as it addresses illness. Traditional medicine (also known as allopathic medicine) addresses the symptoms of a disease, so the treatment begins when the patient gets sick. In the mind–body–spirit model, preventing illness is as important as healing it.

The Covenant Connection

When we want to address physical symptoms, understanding our covenants can be one way of treating ourselves. Changing our covenants will help us understand how our law-based agreements have influenced decisions we have made that may have contributed to our ill health. If we have a covenant to always serve others, for example, then we may neglect our own self-care. Or, if we have a promise that keeps us working hard to gain recognition, we may force our way past the first warning signs of illness. I remember hearing Olympic skater Scott Hamilton describe his experience of trying to "muscle his way" through a pain in his abdomen that was eventually diagnosed as testicular cancer. Hamilton was able to recover, and he has become a spokesperson for early cancer detection and for listening to your body's warning signs.

Stress

A faith-based covenant is a customized stress-buster. The connection between stress and increased incidence of illness has been well documented. Stress emerges at different times and in different ways for everyone. Some people get tense when there is too much to do; others feel anxious when facing an unscheduled day. Some people point to family responsibilities and say they feel the weight of the world on their shoulders; others feel a tightening in their stomachs when they face a heavy work load, money issues, or a problem that they cannot resolve. If stress is caused by so many different things and shows up in so many ways, how can there be one way to address it?

In my work I have seen people try a variety of ways to manage stress. Healing your covenant is a customized stress-buster!

When we create faith-based covenants, we are able to make choices that reflect our true, authentic selves. This gets right to the core of stress. Though the pace and stimulation of our daily lives is easy to blame as the cause of stress, my patients have shown me otherwise. As I see them identify their law-based covenant and create faith-based agreements, it becomes clear to me that it is actually the experience of being out of touch with their true selves and disconnected from a Higher Power that is at the root of most of their stress.

Our faith-based covenant ushers in an authentic, empowered relationship with God; it also invites us to integrate our Promise Breakers into our everyday lives. When we no longer deny them, we live with more balance and flexibility. When I am working with clients who have healed their covenant and they report on a stressful situation, they usually do so with the approach that this, too, shall pass. They have learned to roll with the ups and downs of life, accepting that there are some things they can change and some they cannot. The way they get to this place of acceptance is different for each person because it is based on the nature of their faith-based covenant with God.

I am reminded of the Serenity Prayer:

> God, grant me the serenity to accept things that
>   I cannot change,
> Courage to change the things I can,
> And the wisdom to know the difference.

This prayer is familiar to many people, especially those who have sought support through Alcoholics Anonymous or similar groups. When we heal our covenants, the alignment we develop with our Higher Power provides us with a strong foundation and the kind of inner solace we need for acceptance, courage, and wisdom.

Covenants and the Mind–Body–Spirit Model

I know that to believe the links between identifying our covenants and creating health is a leap of faith for some. It means we must consider that whatever goes on in the mind and spirit can have an impact on the body. For some readers, this may be a concept still under consideration. For others, it is clearly the way healing works. I base much of my work on this premise, so before we get much further I want to offer some thoughts on the mind–body–spirit connection.

It is important to remember that the mind–body–spirit connection is as ancient as healing itself. We lost it in the Western world only about 400 years ago, when French philosopher René Descartes started the scientific revolution, separating mind and body along the way. In many cultures, the mind-body-spirit connection is still the primary model. At the California Pacific

Medical Center, we host a number of teachers from around the world, so I have witnessed or heard about healing modalities from all corners of the earth: Asia, the South Pacific, the Caribbean islands, and South America, as well as from Native American medicine men and women.

I was reminded of how the mind-body connection is alive and well in other cultures when we hosted Yeshi Dhondon, who was once the personal physician to His Holiness, the Dalai Lama. After delivering a lecture on Tibetan medicine, he was asked by one of our students to describe how the body, mind, and spirit work together in healing. Dr. Dhondon paused, and in his gentle demeanor asked the student to repeat himself. He heard the student a second time and then shook his head. "I do not understand this question," he replied.

For Dr. Dhondon, there is no distinction between these elements. It is not as if there are segments of our being with names such as mind or body or spirit. We are one whole being, and in his health model, it is the entire being who is treated.

When the Patient Is Cured
But the Illness Remains

In the late 1970s and early 1980s, I was the chaplain in a leading psychiatric center in the Midwest. It was a sobering time for psychiatry, as those in the field had just spent a couple of decades mastering the miracles of psychotropic drugs and were now having to deal with their limitations. In the late 1950s and early 1960s, the success of lithium, chlorpromazine (Thorazine), and other psychotropic drugs appeared to offer a cure for mental illness. Imagine being a doctor who witnessed the transformation of patients who were once secluded in an "activities" room day after day and could now navigate on their own, outside the safety of the institution. The impact of these drugs was stunning. The doors to these institutions were thrown open, and the patients were released to go out into the world and create productive lives. It was as if they were actually cured.

The trouble was that these drugs—which are a blessing to those in need, as are the generations of psychotropic drugs that have followed—did not cure the illness. They were able to interact with the body's chemistry in ways that had never been seen before, and when they did this successfully, the symptoms of the illness no longer dominated the patient's life. But the illness itself was still there.

Some of the patients who were released into caring situations were able to rebuild their lives. But for many, the scientific approach to curing mental illness fell short. Those who came from traumatic or desperate situations needed counseling to help them beyond what the drugs could do for them chemically. They needed assistance with coping in the world—a safety net of people including their families, therapists, and doctors. Ultimately, they needed to be able to take their prescribed medication, which can be a very difficult task for the mentally ill.

This example is proof that the incredible discoveries of science and medicine are hindered when the person is treated simply as a body without considering emotions and lifestyle in the healing equation.

Mind–Body–Spirit in Everyday Healing

I now see the mind–body–spirit model of treatment come to life every day. The purpose of the Institute for Health and Healing, according to our mission statement, is to "awaken individuals and communities to the deepest meaning of health and the broadest understanding of healing." The physicians at the institute incorporate a discussion of spirituality into their intake sessions with patients. I then sit down with the patients and their physicians to review how patients describe their life purpose and whether their quest for meaning is being fulfilled or lies dormant. This allows us to understand the context in which the patient is experiencing symptoms. If there was a recent crisis in a patient's life, for example, the ways in which the patient is managing it are taken into account before recommending treatment.

I also work with patients who want to explore their covenants, helping them to identify the spiritual promises they made years ago and still adhere to unwittingly. We find that our patients' earliest covenants have a huge impact on their ability to handle stress, to ask for help, and to integrate whatever treatments or lifestyle changes they need to regain their health. By gaining awareness of their covenants, our patients are better equipped to respond to the healing strategies we propose.

Multiple Stresses, Multiple Symptoms: Carol's Story

Carol was in her mid-50s when she contacted us. She had already been to a number of doctors, and brought a file packed with their diagnoses. According to her paperwork, Carol suffered from chronic fatigue syndrome, asthma, irritable bowel syndrome, and depression. When the physician conducting the session asked her what her hobbies were, Carol answered, "doctors' appointments."

Carol's symptoms were real, of course, and we treated her for the discomfort they brought her. But though the problems were manifesting in her body, I believed that the solution might be found in Carol's covenant. It seemed to me that she was traveling from one diagnosis to another, as if she were on a journey that involved having an illness instead of following a path toward health. When I asked her what she envisioned for herself in the near future, she told me she imagined herself getting sicker.

"Why?" I asked. This was unusual, as most people who seek medical help hope to get better and try to hold an image of wellness for themselves.

"Because I'm not ready to change," Carol responded.

I heard her willingness to be candid as a positive sign, and asked her to spend a few counseling sessions with me as part of her treatment. As we began to work together, she talked about conflicting messages she received in childhood. On one hand, she was warned about becoming "too successful," as that would not look good for a girl. Unfortunately, this was not an uncommon message for young women to hear when Carol was a child. On the other hand, her parents stressed the importance of appearance and were especially critical of Carol when she did not create a well-groomed, feminine appearance. In other words, it was not acceptable to be successful in any area except presentation—and there, she was expected to be the best.

As an adult, Carol followed her parents' guidance until her mid-30s, when she decided to pursue a degree in computer programming. She spent the next 20 years working in a high-technology field, where her intelligence was valued much more than her appearance. She talked at length about the satisfaction her profession gave her, but also described feeling pulled in half, as she was ambivalent about becoming too successful. Carol told me of a number of cases where she left a company just as a promotion was about to come her way. In her profession people routinely change companies, but in her case the moves always came just as she was about to be recognized for her accomplishments, and that seemed to me to be important. I wondered if she left her medical treatments as soon as they got close to succeeding as well.

I gave Carol an assignment to write a list of her Promise Breakers as if she were drawing a tree. She was to write the first Promise Breaker that came to mind on the tree itself, and then fill up the root system with any others she could think of. Every-thing she felt was a Promise Breaker would fill up the page, but we could pretend that they were hidden under the earth. This way, the beautiful tree with one simple Promise Breaker is all that would appear.

Carol brought the drawing in the next time we met. She was as proud of it as a child might be, and I could tell she had taken some risks in doing it. The Promise Breaker she wrote across the trunk of the tree read, "be successful." This did not surprise me, as we had talked at length about it. The roots were packed with things she believed she could not do: appear sloppy, act silly, be bossy, loud, funny, or sexy, just to name a few. Carol was enthu-siastic about the experience of doing the exercise, so we talked a little bit about each Promise Breaker. Then I sat back and allowed each of us to be quiet for a moment. Carol held the drawing on her lap, watching me expectantly.

"Now I would like you to choose your Promise Breaker," I told her. "I want you to commit to just one."

This was the beginning of our most fruitful work together. That afternoon, it was impossible for Carol to make the com-mitment. She came to discover that it was also unthinkable for her to commit to her medical treatment, her success, or, in fact, to her appearance. It turned out that success was not the Promise Breaker for Carol. Being successful caused her anxiety, but it did not break her covenant.

Commitment was her Promise Breaker. Carol had taken the conflicting messages from her parents and made an agreement with God that she would make peace with these messages by not fully committing to either one. Over the years, this became a covenant that kept her on the move, never committing to any-thing, including her own health. Carol needed to learn how to commit to herself as the first step in her healing process.

Carol's story illustrates what happens when we treat the whole person instead of just the illness. Her realizations did not specifically reduce her symptoms, but they were not meant to. Instead, by understanding her inability to make a commitment in any part of her life, Carol recognized that this was behind the search she was on for the right doctor and the perfect cure. She could see that, in fact, she had worked with a number of good doctors, but her fear of commitment—and the success that commitment can bring—kept her moving.

Carol's symptoms are much better. She still struggles with illness, but she sticks to the regime we worked out and no longer sabotages her treatment. Now she approaches the healing journey with a new faith-based covenant. The covenant states, *When I am committed to seeing things through to success, I am closer to my Higher Power.*

Alternative Healing and Spirituality

I want to note that just because a patient explores the mind–body–spirit treatment model does not suggest that his or her relationship with his or her Higher Power is any more authentic than those who might prefer conventional medical treatments. At the same time, a commitment to spirituality does not necessarily indicate a willingness to try a holistic approach to healing. I say this because it is easy to confuse the two, especially because of the ways in which "alternative" healing is sometimes marketed, as if a non-Western method of healing brings the patient some kind of contemplative advantage. Spirituality can be part of healing no matter what method you choose.

This understanding is critical in terms of covenants because those of us who are open to the mind–body–spirit model can fool ourselves into believing that our visits to the acupuncturist or the massage therapist will meet our spiritual needs. I agree that maintaining health, celebrating wellness, and honoring our bodies is a rich part of being in tune with our spirit—after all, the body is a temple of God. But God, or our Higher Power, reaches beyond our bodies and into our souls. Different therapies can support us on our spiritual path, but they are not the path itself.

Healing with Grace

When I was learning to write sermons in divinity school, we were taught about two genres. The first is a law sermon, in which it is suggested to parishioners that they may have to change something about themselves to earn God's approval. The second is the grace sermon, which affirms God's immense and unconditional love, leading us to honor it with loving actions.

With a law-based, unconscious covenant, we are embroiled in a belief that we are constantly being judged by God or being held to an agreement by a powerful higher authority. When we change our covenant, we live in a more authentic, empowered relationship with God. This feeling of alignment with our Higher Power can give us the kind of internal support we need to manage the ups and downs of everyday life, reducing the incidence of stress-related illnesses. And, if we do become sick, the balance and mindfulness of a faith-based covenant means we are better prepared to respond.

PART TWO

Balancing Your Promise

CHAPTER 4

Determining Your Covenant Style

Your vision will become clear only when you look into your heart. Who looks outside, dreams. Who looks inside, awakens.

—*Carl Jung*, Psychological Types

Now that you know the importance of understanding and healing your covenants, the next step is to determine what they are and how to change them. Take a look at the Covenant Styles Questionnaire in Chapter 1. Though there are as many covenants as there are people and their relationships with God, over the years I have observed that three styles—Givers, Wanters, and Searchers—can often help determine a person's original covenant.

You will probably recognize aspects of each style in your day-to-day behavior, but as you read through this chapter you will begin to understand which one is most prominent. It is important to understand which style resonates for you because it is a direct result of your spiritual agreement. Once you understand your style, you are on the track to identifying your covenant:

Givers—Givers are most comfortable helping others.

Wanters—Wanters are driven to succeed and yearn for recognition.

Searchers—Searchers move from one thing to the next, trying to find the right place, person, or belief.

One way to think about your style is as a fun-house mirror, distorting through your behavior the conditional agreement you have with God. When you made a promise with God or the Creative Force, you saw the world in the either-or perspective that children use and then unwittingly developed behaviors that provided a way for you to fulfill your covenant. These behaviors led you to tend more toward the style of giving, wanting, or searching. Like most of us, you kept your style in place over the years because it allowed you to be true to your agreement on an unconscious level. Thus, once you determine which style best describes your choices, you can easily hone in on your covenant. When you change your covenant, you will gain access to all of the styles instead of favoring just one. It is the ability to move freely from one style to another, basing your choices on what you need instead of what is defined as acceptable by your covenant, that will provide flexibility and balance.

Taking the Covenants Style Questionnaire is just the first step in discovering if you are a Giver, a Wanter, or a Searcher. To get a better sense of your style, I list 10 questions that define and differentiate them. You may find a number of thoughts stirring as you begin to consider what your style might be, so I repeat the descriptions in an exercise format for you to use with your journal. Chapters 5, 6, and 7 go into considerable detail about each style, and include stories of people who exemplify the styles. My clients often identify themselves as one style when they initially take the questionnaire and read about how each style differs, but then realize they are another once they understand the styles on a more detailed level. I invite you to approach this analysis with an open mind and a willingness to be surprised.

1. How do you respond to stress?

Your style is rooted in stress, so this is where it shows up the most. You became a Giver, a Wanter, or a Searcher when there was disharmony in your childhood home. For example, if you felt the only way to get the love you needed was to help out, you may have promised God that you would always give, as you knew this was the way to secure love. And now, if you are a Giver, you most likely respond to a stressful situation by trying to help.

Covenants are rooted in the family, but they are projected onto God. Therefore, we default to the style that keeps us true to our covenant until we heal old spiritual agreements.

Stress is also an important part of understanding your covenants because when you favor a particular personality style, you are living out of balance. You may not know it, but every moment you are managing the tension that is created by this imbalance. When you create your faith-based covenant, you ease this internal tension. In the face of external stressors such as traffic snarls and work deadlines, you still need to manage stress, but when you are more at ease within, this becomes a simpler challenge.

If you are a Giver, you probably respond to stress by taking care of others. When life gets tough, Givers get helpful.

If you are a Wanter, you may live with a gnawing sense of anxiety or irritation. When things get tough, Wanters start working.

If you are a Searcher, you may have difficulty tolerating stress. When things get tough, Searchers simply get going.

2. *Who do you blame?*

Here's another way the styles differ. When some of us confront a problem, we blame ourselves, but for others the problem is always the fault of another person. Of course, some of us would rather just not deal with the issues of fault or accountability at all.

Where you put the blame can offer great insight into your style and will also help you to understand why other people respond the way they do.

If you are a Giver, you may tend to blame yourself when things go wrong, even if the situation is totally out of your hands.

If you are a Wanter, you blame others. When there is a problem, you will contribute to the solution, and if a crisis hits, you will persevere until everything is resolved. But during it all, you will pin the blame on someone or something outside of yourself.

If you are a Searcher, you do not blame anyone. Blaming requires the ability to be certain who is at fault, and certainty is not something that comes easily to you.

3. *How do you ask for help?*

The way you ask for help is tied directly to your style. Some of us have no problem asking for support. Others expect our loved ones to recognize when we need their help and simply provide it, as if they can read our minds.

I can guarantee that some of you read the question and said, "I don't ask for help. I never would." If this sounds like you, your refusal to ask for help may work when life is going well, but once you are faced with a crisis you could be risking your health and well-being. If your conditional covenant is based on helping others, for example, asking for support forces you to make a choice. You must break the covenant to accept the help.

> *If you are a Giver,* you find asking for help to be a big challenge. In fact, it is impossible for you to do so, and it is one of the primary things you will learn to work on when creating a new covenant.

> *If you are a Wanter,* you have trouble asking for help directly, as you might appear to be needy, which would be intolerable.

> *If you are a Searcher,* you are not shy about asking for help, listening to advice, or trying out new solutions. In fact, it is in asking and trying that you find comfort.

4. *How did your parents relate to you during your childhood?*

If you have siblings, do you think you are all the same style? Chances are you aren't, even though you all had the same parents. If you have ever had the opportunity to discuss your formative years with your brothers, sisters, or anyone else who was a part of this time in your life, you may know that it can be astounding to hear the way they describe your childhood home. It can appear as if you were all brought up in different houses.

You need to focus on how you remember your parents relating to you—not on the stories you hear from others, or how you understand their behavior looking back on it now. Unlike people who were raised in the same families, I have observed that people who share the same styles often describe memories of their parents in similar ways. This is what to consider when you look at how covenants and styles are tied to childhood.

When you think about this question, it is also important to keep your childhood point of view. From the vantage point of adulthood, you may know that your parents tried their best to be warm and loving, but if you did not feel that growing up, this is what you need to be aware of. Or you may now be grateful for the encouragement they provided, but as children their hope for your success may have come across in ways that felt threatening or punitive. For the sake of healing your covenants, it is the memory that matters.

> *If you are a Giver,* you remember that love was conditional in your childhood home, based on how much you gave or on how you helped or served others.

> *If you are a Wanter,* you may have experienced your parents as distant and at times unreliable.

> *If you are a Searcher,* you remember a loving home, but one in which there was little emphasis on focus, follow-through, or accomplishments.

5. *How do you relate to God?*

We explored this question in Chapter 2 when we talked about the definition of spirituality as a reflection of our relationship with God. Every individual has his or her own spiritual path and relationship with God, but people within each style have a tendency to share similarities. In fact, your style can be so hardwired to your definition of faith that when you understand it, you might gain clarity about your beliefs as well. This gives your sense of spirituality great strength, as you can then live in a way that better reflects your deepest, most authentic relationship with God.

> *If you are a Giver,* you believe that God will love you only on the condition that you take care of others.

If you are a Wanter, you experience God as someone or something in the distance whose job is to bring a feeling of spirituality to you.

If you are a Searcher, you relate to God as a seeker, as you are always looking for another way to understand the divine.

6. What is your Promise Breaker?

When you think about your individual Promise Breaker, it is useful to know that each style has its own. As you consider what yours might be, I want to warn you that you may find yourself drawn to a certain Promise Breaker because it looks like a familiar problem. If this happens, watch out—a Promise Breaker you are familiar with could be a decoy. It may be a common problem, or it may be something you need to resolve, and it is always wise to be conscious of this. A Promise Breaker is most often cut off from your awareness, so you will not recognize it as something you need to work on—at first, anyway. How could you recognize something you could not bear to face or have simply refused to see?

I have a client who was convinced she fit the style of a Giver. I could tell after a few meetings that Paula was more of a Wanter, but she thought otherwise. It was when we began talking about the Promise Breaker that a lightbulb went off for her, as she kept "forgetting" what her Promise Breaker would be. All Givers have their own versions of Promise Breakers, of course, but all of them are rooted in the idea of speaking up for one's own needs. When we talked about the Promise Breakers, Paula thought she was a Giver because she had struggled with issues related to speaking up for herself.

The very fact that Paula could look fairly at all angles of the Giver's Promise Breaker showed me that this was not where her healing would begin, and the same could be true for you. It's important to recognize the part of you that you have turned your back on—the part that you feel is truly unthinkable. As we continued to work together, Paula told me that she spent days mulling over the attributes of the Wanter, but when she got to the Promise Breaker she'd have to stop whatever she was doing in order to remember what it was. She realized that the fact that she kept getting to such unknown territory was a sign that this may be exactly where her healing could take place.

For Wanters, the Promise Breaker is based on vulnerability. Vulnerability is not something you allow yourself to experience. As we worked together, Paula recognized that there were times she could not speak up for herself, but the thing she really could not do was appear needy—which is more about vulnerability than about asking for support.

This realization allowed Paula to understand the need to integrate the Wanter's Promise Breaker into her life. She recognized how much more this Promise Breaker brought her closer in her relationship with God than a Giver's would have. Once you can zero in on your Promise Breaker, it will become clear that the very thing you have closed the door on may open another for a healthier life.

> *If you are a Giver,* your Promise Breaker may be focused on finding your own voice and speaking up for what you need.

> *If you are a Wanter,* your Promise Breaker is to be vulnerable. For most Wanters, vulnerability is not just uncomfortable—it is not even a choice to consider.

> *If you are a Searcher,* your Promise Breaker is commitment. Commitment requires the Searcher to take a stand.

7. *How do you look for love?*

Some of us want to be swept off our feet; others want to do the sweeping. Those kinds of differences are often easy to spot. But there are subtle differences in the ways we look for love as well.

Where one style may look for acceptance, another seeks unconditional love. Some of us might want to join our soul mates in their lives; others will assume that our mates will leave their lives behind and join ours.

If you are a Giver, you experience love as serving, nurturing, and taking care of others. You sometimes don't realize that your needs are relevant when you are in relationships.

If you are a Wanter, you look for love through recognition. You probably feel loved when others see you and understand you.

If you are a Searcher, you are good at looking for and finding love. You know that the experience of falling in love is one of the things you constantly seek. As soon as your partner wants commitment, however, you usually look elsewhere.

8. What is your life prayer?

As we've discussed, the life prayer is the thought that rises to the surface as soon as we open our eyes in the morning, and it guides us, whether we realize it or not, throughout our day.

If you are a Giver, you pray to be able to help others—to manage your day in such a way that you can be available to those who need you.

If you are a Wanter, you probably wake up with a long list of tasks and carry a sense of urgency to see them all through.

If you are a Searcher, your life prayer is to keep going, to find a new path, to be led to new discoveries.

9. What is success for you?

It's not as if the styles only show up in our fears and yearnings. The styles also experience success and happiness differently.

If you are a Giver, you feel successful when you know you have made a difference. When you see the positive impact of your service, you feel all is right with the world.

If you are a Wanter, you most likely create a number of occasions that feel successful. You are driven by your need for recognition, as the acknowledgment generated by success can feel like the love you so badly desire.

If you are a Searcher, you excel at start-ups and can often ride the turbulence of a new business or venture better than anyone else. This is where you are most productive, and where your satisfaction is greatest.

10. What style is your partner?

As you read about the styles, you may come across some behaviors that you recognize as belonging to your significant other or a close friend. You may find it easier to understand and support your partner once you know his or her style.

If your partner is a Giver, the trick to keeping the connection healthy and balanced is to encourage your partner to meet his or her own needs.

If your partner is a Wanter, he or she needs to feel that it is okay to be open and trusting with you. Let your partner know that you accept and understand him or her no matter how weak or needy he or she appears.

If your partner is a Searcher, your life will be rich with a sense of adventure, which may be what you want in a relationship. If you want a long-term commitment, however, you may want to take a close look at your choice.

Write Down the Answers for Finding Your Spiritual Style

Now it's time to get a better feel for each of these styles and how they relate to your life. We will revisit each of the 10 areas I just described, but this time around we'll look at these questions practically, in terms of your own life, rather than theoretically. Please have a journal or a pad of paper at your side for writing your answers. Before we start, here are a few ground rules:

- There are no right or wrong answers.
- These are your private thoughts. You do not need to share this exercise with anyone—it's your choice.
- You can take as much time as you need to answer a question.
- Your answers can be long or short.
- You are definitely allowed to go back and cross out.
- You can start over.
- If you find yourself frustrated with any particular question, don't skip it. Instead, try writing about the frustration.
- If you find yourself pleased by what you write, try writing about what that feels like.
- Many find their most fruitful work is done when they first start writing, so approach each question with an open mind and write whatever comes up.
- Others find the most telling and useful material at the end of their journaling. If this is the case with you, when you think you are finished with your answer, write five more words or fill up five more lines, or take another five minutes and see what comes to mind.

1. How do you respond to stress?

I suggest you look at this question in two ways. First, think about how you respond to stress now, as an adult. Do you shut down? Do you get angry? If you get angry, are you upset with yourself or with others? Take some time to write about what you do in the face of stress.

Second, think about your childhood home. How was tension and disharmony expressed? How did you respond to stress in your family? Many children act out stress through illness, fighting, or even excelling in their studies, as success in school can channel the frustrations of home.

2. Who do you blame?

Many of us may not have asked ourselves this question before, as most of us assume that whomever we blame is the one who is at fault. I am asking you to step back for a minute to consider whether you have the same assumption. If you really think about it, do you blame yourself or do you point the finger at other people?

3. How do you ask for help?

Again, this may be a question you have never posed to yourself, as you may not even know that asking for help is an option in your life. I want you to pause for a moment and ask yourself this question: Do you ask for help at all?

If you don't, your assignment is to write about why, and what might happen if you did.

If you are someone who can ask for help, how do you do it? Are you able to directly request support, or do you hint around, hoping that others will see your need? When you are clear on this answer, go a little deeper and think about whether you get the help you truly need. If you do, what do you bring to the request that makes getting the help possible? If you don't, what could you do differently to change this problem?

4. How did your parents relate to you during your childhood?

Here are some points to work with and questions to consider as you explore your thoughts:

- Describe the way your parents related to you, exploring your memories of how they expressed their happiness and their pride, their sadness and their anger.

- How did they demonstrate their feelings for you? Were they affectionate and warm, did they keep a polite distance, or do you remember longing for their attention?

- How did they oversee your behavior and enforce discipline? Were they stern, fair-minded, easygoing, or a little bit of everything?

- Were your parents consistent in the way they related to you or did you always wonder what was coming next?

- All parents experience stress, so include your recollections of how they responded when faced with tension or difficulties.

- Try writing a page about your childhood home in the voice of another family member.

Some of us have mixed feelings about exploring our childhood. This can be an aspect of denial, as revisiting the dysfunction of our families might seem threatening. It can also be a sign of forgiveness or maturity, because many of us believe that our parents did the best they could. Whatever your objections or fears, try to stay present with what it feels like to evoke these memories and record your feelings in your journal. They will be valuable to revisit later on.

If you have sought out healing work on these issues already, you will most likely be surprised at how they may resurface when you identify your covenant. The thing to remember is that looking at your childhood is not about finding out what your parents did right or wrong. In fact, it is not even about what literally occurred at home. It is the way you made sense of the way your parents related to you, because that is at the root of your law-based agreement with God.

5. How do you relate to God?

You might want to look back at the exercises you did in Chapter 2 as you approach this question. If your idea of a Creative Force or a Higher Power transcends a conventional deity, does it feel like a loving, protective spirit?

Think about how God treats you. Are you threatened by judgment, or does God forgive and cherish you no matter what your trespass is?

A number of my clients describe a sense of oneness among all life forms, and they embrace this as their spirituality. I can deeply relate to the powerful connection they describe.

As I talk to some of these clients, however, it seems to them to be a mystical presence apart from themselves. It turns out that they do not feel welcomed by this universal energy, nor are they inspired to be stewards of it.

These are the kinds of things that define your relationship with God. We all live with this connection day in and day out, and it has a tremendous influence on the choices that make up our lives, but we don't always see it. Understanding the way you relate to your Higher Power will not only help you identify your style and create your new covenant, but it can shed light on the way you think about your everyday world.

6. What is your Promise Breaker?

Here's a suggestion for exploring your Promise Breaker: Draw a line down the middle of a blank page, creating two columns. In one column, write a list of things that might be your Promise Breaker—the things you really cannot do. In the other, make notes about what would happen in your life if you were to do each one of them. Would your spouse leave you? Would you feel ashamed? Would you experience emotions that you would prefer to avoid, such as fear, rejection, or loss? Would you lose God's love?

Remember, this is simply an exercise to stir your thoughts. Whatever you write down can change as you begin to heal your covenants. Whatever you name as your Promise Breaker now may not be the one you use when you get to the point of creating a faith-based covenant. You can use this exercise to explore all kinds of thoughts without being attached to any of them.

7. How do you look for love?

This question goes beyond what you look for in another person, asking instead what you look for in the experience of being with that person. Think about what you yearn for when your heart is aching for love. Do you want to feel taken care of or do you want to do the caretaking? Are you comfortable in a relationship that shares power equally, or do you look for a situation in which your partner just takes the reins or asks you to take them? Do you want to fit your life into another's or have your partner's life fit into yours? What feels more like love to you: recognition or adoration?

8. What is your life prayer?

What is the prayer you wake up with? How do you think it might seal your covenant? Knowing your prayer will help you understand your style because its purpose is to affirm your covenant, which in turn is at the root of your style. In other words, as your prayer seals your covenant, your covenant drives your style. When you change your covenant and are able to balance all three styles, your life prayer will also change.

9. What is success for you?

When you have completed a major project in the workplace, do you feel satisfaction just knowing your work stands on its own or do you wait for the recognition of co-workers before your accomplishment really hits home? Does your work have to benefit others in order to be successful, do you judge your success on the reward you earn, or are you glad just to be crossing tasks off your list? These are just a few of the ways that people define success. When you write about what success is for you, give some thought to how you arrived at this feeling. If you look back to your childhood, did you experience success in the same way? Are you satisfied with the way you experience success or would you like to change something?

10. What style is your partner?

Knowing the style of your partner is not an indicator of your own style, but it can provide a way for you to better understand your partner and can offer insights into the kind of support he or she needs.

Identifying Your Style

Before we close our journals, I want you to open to another blank page. I know you have been only briefly introduced to the styles, but you may already have an inkling of which you are— though don't be surprised if you end up changing your mind once you read through Chapters 5, 6, and 7. Feel free to look back at the Covenants Style Questionnaire to see how your answers might already be changing before you go on. Fill in the following two sentences:

1. In terms of my style, I am a _____.

2. I believe this is my style because as long as I _____ _____, then I know that God or my Higher Power will _____.

One thing to note about the three styles is that it is the fact that we default to giving, wanting, and searching that is key, not the outcomes. For example, it does not matter whether Givers offer time, money, or emotional support. The issue is their need to give. No matter how much love and recognition Wanters are offered, it will not be experienced as enough until they change their covenant. For Searchers, the places that searching takes them are inconsequential. It is the seeking itself that keeps them connected to their covenant.

As you filled out the assessment and read through these descriptions, you may have recognized different parts of yourself reflected in each style. We will look at how we often blend the styles in Chapter 8. You may tend toward being a Giver in relationships, but when you go to work you may feel like a full-fledged Wanter. If this is the case, how do you determine which style to focus on to understand your covenant?

That's where the questions in this chapter come in. Understanding the ways you respond to stress, look for love, or experience success, just to name a few, will direct you past the style you have adapted to fit social or professional circumstances and point to the interior one you developed as a child. Then the process of creating a new faith-based covenant can begin.

Finally, the important thing to remember as you read the next three chapters is that these styles do not define who you are. When you recognize yourself in one of the styles, this does not mean it is your destiny to always personify the style—far from it. Once you identify your style and determine your own faith-based covenant, you are free to both honor the strength of your style and to make choices according to what is happening in your life right now—not according to a spiritual agreement you made years ago.

CHAPTER 5

The Promise of the Giver

Our deepest fear is not that we are inadequate. Our deepest fear is that we are powerful beyond measure. It is our Light, not our darkness that most frightens us. We ask ourselves, who am I to be brilliant, gorgeous, talented and fabulous? Actually, who are you not to be? You are a child of God. Your playing small doesn't serve the world . . . as we let our own Light shine, we unconsciously give other people permission to do the same.

—*Attributed to Marianne Williamson,* A Return to Love: Reflections on the Principles of a Course in Miracles

I know I am talking to a Giver when I hear the person explain how much he or she does for other people. It is as if they have set up a conditional agreement that says, *As long as I give to others, God will love me.*

This agreement has a different tone, of course, depending on the person. Some of the versions I hear are that life will work out—or God will love me—as long as:

- I care for others
- I don't think of myself too highly
- I work hard
- I get a lot of things done
- I give more than I receive

Let me say right away that caring for others is without question a wonderful thing. As a chaplain, I honor the value of service on its deepest level, as it is often in service to others that we can feel closest to God or can feel most aligned with our Higher Power. For many, reaching out beyond ourselves to touch the lives of others is a spiritual act, since it is a way to be a part of our community. Some say that helping others keeps them alive, as it gives them an authentic sense of unity. And giving in a generous, mindful way is actually nurturing, as it feeds the soul to be connecting to another in this way.

The rub is that Givers are often unable to make choices that are not based on serving others. What looks like giving is actually like getting stuck on a wheel in a hamster cage. All of your giving keeps you active, so it feels as if you are moving forward, but in fact you are running in place. You may not realize you are on this wheel, but you feel exhausted from its constant spin.

Givers are most likely to be women. There are men who give too much as well, and I include a few examples of men in this chapter to illustrate this point. But our culture has glorified an image of the nurturing woman to such a degree that even the most independent-minded women often find themselves drawn to giving. Broadly speaking, most men simply do not face the societal pressures to be caring and nurturing as women do.

Givers and Stress: "I Can Help"

As we discussed in Chapter 4, the circumstance in which your style will be most prominent is in the way you respond to stress, as that is how you initially developed it. When things were too overwhelming, you were drawn to a particular style to make sense of your world. If you are a Giver, you most likely made sense of your world by being a good helper. Now when things get stressful, you help out. You try to fix the situation. You try to be a good helper, because as a child you did such a good job and got so many rewards for this role that now it seems as if this is who you are.

The truth is that giving is a strong, valuable part of you, but it is not all of you. Most Givers have a powerful inner voice that is still waiting to be heard.

Givers and Blame: The Inner Blame Game

In the minds of you Givers, no matter what the situation, it is always your fault. The blame and the solution are both on your shoulders. No matter how grave or incidental the problem, if you had only worked harder or cared more, things would be easier all around. Here's a story that illustrates the way you Givers figure out how to blame yourselves, no matter how innocuous the situation.

A group of neighbors often joined forces to help each other out with lawn and house projects. They jokingly called their group the Barn Raisers. These neighbors usually spent an afternoon holding the ladder for somebody fixing a gutter or snapping in storm windows. It was a good way to keep the community connected and to help share the chores.

Three of them went on an errand to a hardware store one Saturday. Two of them were Givers—one of whom was driving—and one was a Wanter. They drove to a crowded shopping center, where it was difficult to find a parking space.

"They should have built more spaces," the Wanter said, as they circled the lot.

"Well, I should have left earlier," the Giver who was driving responded.

"I should have reminded you," the other Giver said.

"I can't believe how many people are here," the Wanter sighed. "What do they all need?"

"I wish I had asked you if you needed anything when I went out yesterday," the Giver in the passenger seat said. "Then I could have taken care of this."

"Thanks," the first Giver answered, cruising slowly up and down the aisles, "but this is really my fault. I should have done this during the week."

"They never should have built this shopping center here," the Wanter said.

"I'm sorry," the first Giver responded. "I should have known it would be crowded."

"I just wish I had thought to ask you when I went out yesterday," the other Giver said. "I could have saved you this trip."

"These people should all go home," the Wanter muttered, shaking his head. "Then we'd find a space."

This is a wonderful illustration of how Givers and Wanters respond to the same situation. Both Givers believed that the blame was theirs. Yes, they could have done the errand at a different time, and it was admirable of them to take responsibility for that. But the real point of the story is that it would never occur to them as Givers that the situation was not entirely their fault. Neither one of them created the number of cars, the size of the lot, or the popularity of the store. And they certainly did not create the blame game being played by the Wanter.

It is in these moments of stress that we can often detect our style coming out. Think about how you would respond in the same situation. If you are a Giver, you may have nodded in agreement when one neighbor apologized for not doing the errand earlier in the week. It may be clear to you that the whole thing was her fault. But if you Givers shoulder the responsibility when things go wrong, what do you do when you are the ones who need help? What do you do when you need someone else to bear the burden?

"No Thanks, I'm Fine"

Givers cannot ask for help—in fact, many of you Givers know that when asked if you need anything, you respond, "No thanks, I'm fine." And the truth is that you may actually think you are fine, because in your world you can never be the one who needs help. It is often intolerable for a Giver to be needy.

But let's get real. Everyone needs help from time to time, and even if a Giver does not ask for support, friends and family will step forward to provide it. The problem—and it can be a life-and-death problem—is that as a Giver you are not only unable to ask for help, you are unable to accept it. This can create real difficulties. When you become sick or face a crisis, for example, you pose a risk to yourself simply because you cannot receive the support that is offered to you.

Keeping the Peace: My Mother's Story

A true Giver, my mother was a source of support to the other women in her neighborhood and her church, listening to their problems and helping them with their families whenever she saw the need. In our house, she kept the peace. She intercepted whatever came through the door and made sure it would not upset my father or interfere with running a smooth, calm household. I surmised that her covenant was *If I keep the peace and hold everything together, God will love me.*

On one hand, the covenant worked for her. She raised her children, kept her husband happy, and ran her home with few disruptions. She was cherished for all the help she gave to other families. That seemed to be enough for her

But then my mother got sick. In her early 60s, she was diagnosed with cancer. The diagnosis came after several turbulent years. My father had retired, and he was immediately struck by an illness that nearly killed him. We learned later that it was Legionnaires' disease, though at the time no one knew what he had. My mother was at his bedside for months.

When he recovered, they continued with their retirement plans. They bought a new place in Florida for the winter months, and my mother took on the logistics of keeping up one home while creating another. She had just put the finishing touches on their new place when her doctor detected a small tumor during a routine physical exam. Now she was the one who needed the help.

The doctors were confident that a round of chemotherapy would eliminate the tumor. They believed it had not metastasized and gave her a 90 percent chance of recovery. As those of you whose lives have been touched by cancer know, chemotherapy can be horrific. The treatment poisons the cancer cells, but since it cannot always detect which cells are cancerous, other areas of the body are affected as well. Patients may lose their hair or spend days feeling weak and nauseous. My mother was terrified of this.

I was scared, too. As the treatment approached, I realized that I had never seen my mother succumb when she was sick. Even when I was a boy and saw her with the flu, she forced herself out of bed to cook for the family. And I certainly had no memory of my sister, my father, or me ever bringing her a sick tray, though I remembered that my friends helped their mothers when they were not well. When she was diagnosed, I was well along in my career as a chaplain, so I had spent long hours with patients who suffered from cancer. I could not imagine how she would cope with such pain. Hers was a hopeful prognosis, but I still knew what she was about to endure. I felt anxious and powerless.

As fate would have it, my mother received her chemotherapy in the same hospital where I was serving as a pastoral counselor. I was able to visit her often, and I was familiar with the doctors and nurses who attended to her. I felt encouraged whenever I stopped by to see her, as she seemed to be tolerating the treatment quite well. Her doctors agreed, especially in view of what other patients often go through. My mother felt sick, but was not terribly weakened, and she still had a full head of hair.

I was surprised, then, when one of her nurses approached me as I was on my rounds to tell me that she was not doing well. The nurse said that she "wasn't fighting." I knew, though, that my mother always fought back when she was sick. Was this going to be the way she coped? I immediately went to her room.

She looked resolute when I walked in the door, as if she had made up her mind about something and was off in the distance with her decision. As I approached her bed, I felt that my mother was no longer there.

I told her that she was doing well. "You've tolerated the treatment with hardly any side effects," I said, brushing my fingers softly through her hair.

She lay quietly, her eyes focused on the ceiling.

Her silence scared me. If the side effects were her biggest fear and if they were not as bad as we had all expected, then why wasn't she hopeful? I had worked with patients who would have been thrilled with this kind of progress. Had she given up? The thought was unbearable.

"This will be over soon," I said. "You'll get through this and then it will just be a thing of the past. I've seen so many patients get through this, Mom. I know you can, too. Let's just fight this. I know you can."

My mother raised her hand slightly, gesturing for me to stop. She turned her face away, and then back, locking me with her gaze.

"You know, son," she said, "there are worse things than dying."

The chemotherapy eliminated this tumor, but another was found shortly after she came home. My mother refused to get more treatments. All of the people she had reached out to and helped in her life—me, my sister, my wife, Ruth, my father, and all the friends and neighbors she had cared for so genuinely— came to her bedside and surrounded her with love and nurturing. But my mother did not appear to accept the care and support we offered.

The visiting nurses came and went, administering the medication needed to ease the pain, and my mother lay in her bed, ignoring us all. The nurses had a term for this—*cocooning*—which describes what happens when patients marshal all of their energy and turn inward rather than relating to those around them.

But this situation felt different. I felt as if I could see the struggle my mother was in as we all reached out to help her. It was as if she could only feel our love if we gave it in return for her care, and now she was unable to be the caregiver.

As those who have cared for terminally ill people know, there are sometimes simple pieces of equipment that patients refuse to admit needing, as if to do so would be a way of letting the illness win. These things become symbols: the chair in the shower, the bed with railings, the hospital commode. We held off for as long as possible before we brought any of these items into the house. One evening, my father called to let me know that my mother had deteriorated to such a degree that she needed an adjustable mattress, so he ordered a hospital bed and other equipment for her.

The next morning, he phoned again. It was dawn and the sky outside my window was mixed with both the fading stars and the rising daylight. He was calling, he slowly explained, because my mother had passed away that night. In my mind, it was as if her need for a hospital bed was intolerable. It meant she was too sick, too needy, too reliant on others. It meant she had to go.

I hope that my mother died the way she wanted to. I know that cancer is often out of our control, no matter how advanced our technology or how deep our faith. I am a hospital chaplain, which in one respect is like being a foot soldier: You see people die, and you can never know why one person falls and another survives and gets to go home.

But I also know that people who spend their lives giving to others can be paralyzed when it is their turn to receive, and I believe this contributed to my mother's death. I believe that when she told me there were worse things than death, the thing she was talking about was the possibility of being the one who was needy. I believe she could no longer live within her covenant.

If that is the case, I respect her decision. But I don't recommend it for you. If you are a Giver, I suggest you think long and hard about how you will respond when you need help. If it seems impossible, I hope you consider taking a look at your covenant and allowing yourself to ask for help. For some, my story may seem like an exaggeration of how covenants work. But if you are a Giver, you know how true it is.

Givers and Their Parents: Great Expectations

Givers remember their parents as demanding. You Givers may have responded to your parents' needs before they even recognized yours, so you learned early on that your wants and needs were not the most important ones in the household.

You Givers might recall your father having high expectations of you. For many, your mother was also a Giver, and in fact she found most of her connection through serving her spouse. This dynamic sets up a template for giving. As children, you Givers were usually trying to please your father, which was ultimately impossible. If you ran into failure there, you attempted instead to model your mother, creating whatever connection you could by serving. Givers are well trained in listening for and responding to the needs of others.

Givers often describe in one word how they wish their parents had related to them: *acceptance*. You wish you had simply been accepted and loved without any strings attached. Instead, you may remember feeling loved by your parents only on the condition that you reached out to others. This could have been through helping out a neighbor, volunteering in programs that served the poor, or pitching in with household chores within the family. You may have received the message that you were lovable only when you helped others. This may be where you learned to keep your own needs second in line.

Givers and God: God Is Almighty

For Givers, your demanding parent was projected onto God. Your law-based covenant might dictate that you must work hard to take care of others in order to be loved by God. Just as you were not accepted by your parents unless you were giving, you feel you are not accepted by God unless you fulfill this condition.

Do the Right Thing: Taylor's Story

Taylor, one of my students, realized his covenant when he faced a life crisis: *As long as I never disappoint God, God will always love me.* His family attended the Christian Reform Church, a fairly conservative mainstream Protestant denomination. One of the tenets of the church was the importance of appearance, so Taylor learned early on to always behave properly in public. He had not even ordered an alcoholic drink until he was 30, simply because it might not "look good," and this might disappoint God. Because the emphasis was on appearance and on how others viewed him, he could do whatever he wanted in the privacy of his own home as long as the curtains were drawn.

Another way to look good and keep up appearances was to do for others. Taylor was a Giver. He was constantly offering his assistance to people, always doing the right thing by following through with whatever they asked for. Like all Givers, his Promise Breaker was to stand up and say what he really needed.

I met Taylor when I was on the faculty of a doctoral program in pastoral counseling. He was affable and well liked by everyone, but he had a difficult time in the classes that focused on personal feelings. Showing emotions was definitely not a proper thing to do in public, so having to do so as part of school confounded Taylor. He wanted to tow the line, but the line was confronting his beliefs. And then his world turned upside down.

Taylor was married. His wife was as committed to appearances as he was, and on the surface, they were a perfect couple; they prayed together and attended church regularly. But suddenly, and to Taylor's total shock, his wife asked for a divorce. He knew he had done everything right, but she said she did not love him anymore, and she was leaving. It was at this point that Taylor came to the workshops and said he wanted to change.

He talked to the group about the huge difference between being home, when the shades were down, and being out in public. He said that at home he was comical and relaxed. He described the easel he had set up in a spare room, where he often painted just for fun, admitting this as if he were at confession. He said, "I can be whoever I want to be in the privacy of my house, but I have to wear a mask out in public."

He talked about wanting to bring all sides of himself out. It wasn't that he didn't respect decorum, but he was tired of the "oppression of appearance."

This was, in fact, what his wife told him led to her decision to leave the marriage. Though they had originally found a commonality in the need to maintain a positive image, she eventually told Taylor that living with him was a "double dose" of it. She recognized that one of the very things that first attracted her to Taylor—his commitment to status—was now the part of herself she needed to heal and change. On one hand, Taylor wanted to honor her desire to heal, but he also felt at a loss about what his next step would be.

"I just want to be real," he declared at one point, and was then challenged by a classmate to take responsibility and create that for himself.

"If you want to be real, make the choice," she said.

To the group's great pleasure, Taylor took her up on it. He used his statement to create a faith-based covenant for himself that allowed him to balance who he really is with his strengths in creating a good impression or a nice appearance. His new covenant is *As long as I am real, I will be in a more authentic relationship with God.*

The Giver's Promise Breaker: Speaking Up

Imagine a continuum with the word *giving* on one end and its opposite on the other. You Givers might be momentarily stumped when you imagine this continuum. The opposite will be exactly what you need to do to create a healthy balance in your life, but because of your covenant you will have difficulty allowing yourself to see it. The opposite is your Promise Breaker. For

Givers, this is usually related to the idea of standing up and asking for what you want and need. This is the one thing that will break the agreement made to God so long ago.

If you are a person who gives, what does it mean to ask for what you want? And to actually receive it? The reality is that Givers can hardly imagine being cared for just for who they are. This would break the agreement they have with God, because their covenant links doing for others with being loved. For most Givers, the concept of simply being loved without the condition of how much they contribute is mind-boggling.

When I work with Givers, I always see you getting stuck at this place. You can usually see that your caregiving is the only way you can connect to others. You can often speak to issues of trust and abandonment in your childhood that contribute to this belief. You can always discuss the link between spirituality and service. When faced with the idea of asking for what you need, however—something you can rattle off intuitively when done for others—you draw a blank. It means stating that you deserve love for who you are, not for what you do.

You Givers may feel that you want to receive, but the idea of asking for the love that you want to receive is a little too much for you. This is your edge. This is what you have to do. In order to truly receive, you must give voice to the fact that you are owed the same unconditional caring that you offer to others. And you must make the choice to stand up and accept it when it comes your way.

A Covenant in Balance

Most of the stories I include in this chapter focus on people who need to change their covenants, as their journeys help illustrate the process you may be going through. It is important to point out, however, that many people live at peace with a covenant that supports a balanced life and an authentic relationship with their Creative Force.

Leo fit this description. His covenant was based on being fair. As a gay man, he was acutely aware of the way fairness—or a lack of it—could affect one's life. Many of the choices he made in his life revolved around whether everyone was treated with as much equity as possible. The thing that makes Leo different from Charles or my mother, however, is that he was aware of the potential to totally default to his covenant and knew he also needed to include his own needs when considering those of others.

Leo was a transplant patient. He was a recipient of two livers already, but his hepatitis C was so virulent that both had succumbed to the disease within a few years of transplantation. (Hepatitis C is a bloodborne viral disease, so when a person infected with the virus receives a new liver, the disease is not eliminated. The hope is that the healthy liver will tolerate the virus better than the one that has already been ravaged, and, in fact, many liver recipients live for years after transplantation.) His doctors wanted to put him on a waiting list for a third donation, but Leo did not think this was fair. As he saw it, he had been given his chances, and now it was time to offer this gift of life to someone else.

The prospect of dying of liver disease is frightening, of course, and Leo experienced great anguish over this decision. But he also felt his choice came from a place of deep knowing. Refusing a third transplantation was not about giving at the expense of himself. It was about saying what was the truth for him.

Leo was a charismatic man and had a large circle of loyal friends. I stopped by to see him almost every day until he died, and there was always someone there, giving him the care he had offered to so many others when he was well. He was a Giver, but his covenant was in balance. He was able to receive their love in his time of need.

Givers and Love: Love Is Service

You Givers usually look for relationships in which you feel accepted and needed. This allows you a safe way to relate to others, as the connection is based on what you can give, and that's what you know how to do.

As a Giver, your understanding of how to be a partner in a relationship does not include your own needs. If you have recognized yourself in the descriptions of the Giver, it may surprise you to read this—not because it isn't true, but because you never even thought about your needs. The notion may not be in your consciousness. It can be possible, though, when you are ready to make the choice—this is what healing your covenant and realizing the promise of your soul is all about.

But there is risk in change. You may have created a way of relating to others that keeps you from facing unresolved issues involving trust and being taken care of. You know that your generosity can guarantee you a sense of familiarity with others, so why stand up and ask for more? This is not the case for everyone who is in the position of caregiving, of course, as many people choose to nurture others and are also able to experience deep love and intimacy. The key word is *choice*—because Givers are unable to choose to create connection without playing their giving role. But if giving is the way you create relationships, how do you form connections once you choose to change your covenant?

The way most Givers I have worked with learn to foster relationships is to balance their desires to help others with the ability to say what they want and need. Then you have to allow your friends and partners to love you for who you are, not for how much you give. I realize that for many Givers this is like being told you can fly if you jump off the roof and spread your arms. The notion that you could trust your arms to become wings is as absurd as being loved for who you are.

The Giver's Life Prayer: "Help Me to Serve Those in Need"

What are the thoughts you begin your day with? You Givers catalog the needs of others, planning the day around the ways you can make sure that all their needs are met. If your spouse has an important business meeting, you want to remember to call the office afterward. If your child has a sports event, you don't just want to attend—you also want to bring the cooler full of snacks to share with the other parents and kids. If a relative is sick or a friend is feeling down, you make a mental note to drop a card or send a surprise gift.

As I have said before, these are genuine impulses, and when a Giver reaches out in the true spirit of generosity, it feels great. The challenge for you Givers is to be able to discern when your motivation is based on your care for another and when it is a way of maintaining your law-based covenant. When you have no awareness of this distinction, your giving can become a chore. To lose the joy of nurturing others would be comparable to an artist who loses her sight, or a musician whose hearing has faded. It is the way you connect with life. If you keep yourself on automatic pilot when you serve others, you actually risk losing this source of great pleasure.

Givers and Success: "Whatever I Do, It Matters"

"I made a difference." You Givers know the feeling of success that you get when you can say this. You are most satisfied when you know that your contribution to a project had an impact on how things turned out. Your support is genuine, so you are able to experience some of the best feelings in life: love, loyalty, happiness, hope—and when you do for others, you believe that you are sharing these genuine experiences.

When you reach out to help others, you do so because you believe your gesture is important. It might be to volunteer in a classroom, or to help a neighbor wade through mysterious medical forms, or to drop off a warm meal for someone who is housebound. You know that if you did not help, the deed might easily go undone, and in this way you have an impact on the world. In a way, you are lucky. You live without the cynicism and fear that can cripple the best of intentions. You truly believe in doing good—and when you do good, you savor your success.

If Your Partner Is a Giver: Do You Know What Your Partner Needs?

If you are in a relationship with a Giver, it can feel on one level as if you have hit the jackpot. This person will do anything for you. But though it can be easy to get used to this situation, you will not be creating a healthy relationship if you allow the Giver to constantly take care of you. Givers need your support in finding their voice and boundaries. They need to know that you will still be there for them even if they do not take care of you all the time.

Understanding the dynamic that is part and parcel of loving them is a wonderful opportunity for you. It gives you a chance to look at your own motivation. Why do you choose to be with someone who gives? How would your feelings change if the Giver spoke up for his or her own needs? What would happen inside of you if the tables were turned and you took care of the Giver? These are the kinds of questions you will need to face if you want your relationships to deepen, no matter who you are with.

When Givers Create a Faith-Based Covenant

When you Givers choose to create a covenant that brings you closer to your own experience of God, your life opens up in ways you may not have allowed yourself to imagine. In fact, you will discover a new aspect of giving. As you allow your own voice to be heard and your needs to be met, you will be inviting others to give to you. As you receive from them, you will be allowing them to feel the joy of caregiving that you know so well. Receiving can become as rich a form of connection for you as giving, once you are able to choose it. Balancing your impulse to give with the ability to accept will help you to realize the promise of your soul.

CHAPTER 6

The Promise of the Wanter

God said to me, "My grace is sufficient for you, for power
is made perfect in weakness" for whenever I am weak,
then I am strong.

—Paul, 2 Corinthians, Chapter 12, verses 9 and 10

Wanters long to be understood. You yearn for acknowledgment
from others, and to find the right person to love you in just the
right way.

Everyone wants recognition and intimacy, of course. I am a
Wanter, and as someone who has faced this style and continues
to deal with it on a daily basis, I know that we cross our wires,
confusing recognition with love, and love with recognition.
Recognition feels like love. When we look for love, we think the
place to find it is in recognition.

You Wanters do this because you are seeking the recognition and unconditional love you never felt as children. You try to recoup these feelings through the way other people care for you and see you, but that is not where your loss occurred. You Wanters have a tough time recognizing this, so you just keep trying again and again. Your experience of wanting love and recognition dominates your entire way of being in the world. The irony is that you spend so much energy wanting that you rarely find what you need.

The challenge for you Wanters reminds me of the story of a man who lost his car keys. He was looking around the street under a lamppost when a passerby asked if he could help.

"Where exactly did you drop them?" he asked, eyeing the area of light where the man was searching.

The man pointed to the curb several feet away, in the darkness.

"Then why are you looking here?" the passerby asked.

"Because I can't see over there," the man answered.

You Wanters are looking in the only place you can see—and it is also the wrong place. You look for recognition and love in other people, and when you do not get it there—which you never can—you then blame them for your experience of disappointment. You need to examine the role of your own behavior in this disappointment, but to do so never occurs to you. Like the man who has lost his keys, you can't see that you have responsibility for your disappointment, so you just don't look there.

For you Wanters, life can be a series of unmet expectations. Even when you do get what you want, it is never enough. You focus so much time and energy desiring things that you cannot see them when you have them. When you get acknowledgment for your accomplishments and are nourished by others, you do not feel satisfied. You want more. You feel as if no one ever really understands.

You Wanters don't have a handle on your relentless yearning. You have no idea how much this yearning is controlling your life.

It is similar to the way that Givers don't realize they have silenced their own needs in their pursuit of serving others.

You Wanters have an agreement that promises God's love or approval when you feel

- I am cared for in the way I deserve
- I am not taken advantage of
- I am appreciated
- I am understood
- I am recognized

The positive side to being a Wanter is that your pursuit of recognition can lead you to great professional success. Since you never believe that what you have done has earned the validation you want, you keep on trying to find it by doing more. You set your goals, you work hard to reach them, and then you look around to reap the rewards of recognition. But no matter how much people applaud you, you cannot hear it. So you get back in the saddle and try to reach the next goal, since maybe then you will experience the recognition you strive for. Wanters do not give up. As a result, you're terrific at envisioning and realizing goals, and you end up knowing how to achieve almost anything you set your mind to.

When the Cause Is the Community

The drive that Wanters have can be a double-edged sword when it comes to getting recognition. Sometimes the ability to go for your vision is exactly what keeps you from getting the acknowl-edgment and love that you want. You Wanters run the risk of appearing so confident as you lead the way that other people sincerely do not realize you need recognition as much as—if not more than—everyone else. The situation becomes further complicated when you are so clear on what needs to be done to further a cause or achieve a goal that you pursue it at the expense of the connections with those who share your vision.

Sometimes, it is as if the Wanter feels more intimacy for the cause than for the people involved with it. You have a picture in your mind of what it will take to get from point A to point B (or from A to O, as Wanters are usually ambitious) and you can grasp all the details that will need to be accomplished along the way. You honestly think that by keeping this vision alive, you are doing the best thing for everyone. And you are so clear on the mission that you assume everyone else involved in the project is on board in the same way, so you keep your eyes on the prize and go full speed ahead.

In reality, you Wanters know that it is not quite that simple. When you work with a group of people, you need to respect that not everyone can operate on full throttle. But when you are revved up for a cause, you are not able to see this. You Wanters get so much satisfaction from the progress you make toward attaining a goal that if anyone gets in the way, you may feel it is totally reasonable to ask him or her to step aside for the sake of the bigger cause. People get their feelings hurt, or they lose their jobs, or they simply decide that it is too difficult to work with Wanters, and they leave.

You Wanters almost always reach your goal. You learned early on how to jockey for recognition and triumph over obstacles in your way, so you now apply those skills to whatever you set your sights on. An organization that was once faltering is back on its feet, or a vision that people have been working for years to bring to life now stands before you, with a future all its own. As a Wanter, you know that your contribution is essential to the success of the venture, but when you look for recognition you may discover more ambivalence than glory. When you finish the journey, you discover that some important people have been lost along the way.

This shocks you. You think you are doing the best thing for

everyone, but it turns out that getting to the end of the journey is not the only goal. How you get there is important, too. This is difficult for you to believe because of your urgent need for recognition. You can see that the end is in sight, and you can taste the possibility of finally being heralded for the amazing things you have done. At the end of the day, of course, all the success in the world will only feel empty if you are unable to experience the understanding and love that you really want.

Stress and Anger

You Wanters developed your style when you felt you could not trust your parents to recognize, love, and understand you. To you, the love was conditional. This may sound a little like the environment in which the Givers grew up, and in some ways it is. Givers and Wanters grew up in homes with similar dynamics, but each responded in different ways. Whereas Givers made sense of conditional love by earning it through doing good and serving others, Wanters took it as a form of distancing. You felt a lack of connection, as if there were a gap between you and your parents. This was painful, so you tried to fill the void through accomplishments and achievements you hoped your parents would recognize, hedging your bets on the possibility that this would create the connection you longed for. To this day, you Wanters still bet that if you just work harder for your recognition, the vacant feelings you once felt in childhood will be filled to the brim with love.

There's a catch, though. When you felt the lack of love as children, you did not only decide to create connection through your diligence and hard work—you also developed a suspicion that even if you were to find what you wanted it might not be reliable. It might feel like love. But how could you trust this feeling? The way you experienced love from your parents taught you that you really could not count on it. So you work to find intimacy, but when it looks you in the face, you freeze. You are paralyzed by the possibility of having to trust again. That's why it is difficult for you to experience acknowledgment and caring when it comes your way.

What this means in terms of stress is that you walk around with a gnawing level of suspicion. You can't help but believe that someone may take advantage of you or is about to turn on you. For some Wanters, this results in living with the constant companionship of low-grade anger. Sometimes it can flare up into a full-blown rage, but usually it just accompanies you throughout the day, touching almost every personal interaction and permeating your thoughts when you are alone.

When I began to work on my own covenant, I realized that I carried this anger more than I ever imagined. I reacted to little miscommunications personally, as if the intent of an interaction gone awry were to undermine or annoy me. I realize now that I had no other way of seeing it, as the hum of suspicion that is part of the Wanter dominated my listening. When things were out of kilter, I unconsciously perceived the world as a place that was going to betray me once again, and responded with the fear that is expressed as anger. It was only after I understood how mistrust and suspicion infiltrated my view of the world that I recognized this. Before working on my covenant, I did not fully comprehend that stress is merely a part of life. Instead, stress seemed like something concocted just to annoy me.

I realize that I risk painting myself as an irritated, edgy guy. You may have been thinking of yourself as a Wanter, but you know your social persona is amiable, unlike the way I just described my reactions, so you may be reconsidering whether the Wanter is really your style.

It still could be. Though I could get gruff when faced with tension, the truth is that in most situations I maintained an impressive control of my anger and was perceived as someone who was fairly happy with his life. I was determined, but my associates found me inclusive and easy to work with. My days were filled with counseling others, and my anger never surfaced then. I was congenial in most interactions. After all, if I was working so hard for recognition, I did not want it to be for something as shameful as anger.

But underneath it all, I can now see, I felt angry. I could not face my anger head-on, as it would have meant confronting my vulnerability, so I kept it in check as much as possible. If this description of the Wanter resembles your behavior, there is a chance that you, too, could be keeping your anger at bay. You might not know it, because it is the kind of thing that feels so natural that you take it for granted.

Losing Your Edge:
The Surprising Warmth

Have you ever spent a winter in the north and then boarded a plane headed south in February or March for a respite from the cold? I can remember taking breaks when I lived in Michigan, either for business or pleasure, and when I walked out of the airport in Miami, Los Angeles, or Tucson, I would feel absolute surprise when the warmth hit my body. It was as if I did not know I was chilled until I felt the sun against my face. I had gotten so accustomed to bracing against the freezing temperatures that I had lost track of what it felt like to relax.

The same kind of thing happened when I realized that I had been living with a low hum of anger. Once I explored my covenant and was able to recognize my wanting as an adapted style instead of as the way life could be, I was able to see that this anger was no longer relevant for my life. As I healed my covenant, I sometimes experienced the relief of walking into the sunshine after a long winter. The anger I had no idea I was holding dissipated. It occurred to me that I could respond differently now, and I do. When I remember my faith-based covenant, I move through my day more relaxed. I know that when a stressful situation occurs, it is not trying to get me. It is simply stress, there is usually no call for anger, and I only need to respond to the situation at hand.

Because you Wanters might walk around with an undercurrent of anger, adding stress can be like tossing dry kindling across a bed of red-hot embers. Stress can upset all of us, but when you Wanters get tense, you are reminded on a deep level of the hurt and betrayal that have never healed.

Just when you need your resources the most, you can be weakened by your displaced anger or suspicion. If you suffer a minor irritation due to a change in your schedule or some other mundane circumstance, it's just a quirk you can live with. But when you are truly facing a crisis, or if you become sick, your inability to trust others flares up so much that it can become your primary experience. These are the times when you need your power the most, but as a Wanter you run the risk of undermining your best interests by defaulting to suspicion and anger.

This is why it is so important for you Wanters to heal your covenants. Unless you understand all of the choices that are available to you in the face of stress, you will be at the mercy of agreements you made a long time ago.

Wanters and Blame: You Always Know Who Is at Fault

You Wanters look for fault in the same place you look for love and recognition—other people. But, unlike love and recognition, when you look for fault you can easily find it. When in crisis, the idea that you may play a part in the creation and resolution of whatever is going on is the farthest thing from your mind. You need someone else to fix this—*now*.

Do you remember the childhood admonition that if you point your finger at someone else, there will be three more pointing at you? Try pointing at something and you'll see exactly what I mean—the last three fingers on your hand, folded against your palm, are directed back toward you. This is a lesson the Wanter still needs to learn.

How Wanters Ask for Help: "Can't You See I Need You?"

There is an irony in being a Wanter. You want help, but you do not want to be vulnerable. You do not want to open yourself up to the possibility of experiencing the lack of understanding and connection that you felt as a child. In your experience, when you ask for help, it isn't offered to you in a way that you can trust. Therefore, the Wanter thinks that it is better not to ask at all. When you need help, you maintain an image of bravado and you carry on.

Unlike Givers, who don't ask for help because they don't know they deserve it, you Wanters know quite well that you deserve to be helped and supported—you just can't put your feelings into words. That would mean showing your neediness. So what do you do instead? You expect help.

You expect others to help you because you help them. Wanters do not focus specifically on serving others, as Givers do. The way that you Wanters help others is sometimes difficult to see—except to you—because you do so in the course of achieving your goals. When a Wanter champions a cause in the workplace, for example, it almost always gets done. It might be an expansive leadership style that welcomes newcomers into work teams, providing opportunities for people who are often overlooked. It might be a financial decision that directs funds from one project to another in order to keep a small program afloat, or a management system that rewards employees for their incentives.

Whatever it is, you Wanters often help others by using your ability to achieve. But in your quest to be understood and seen, you implicitly assume that when you are the ones in need, others will help you.

The trouble is that most people, understandably, do not recognize it when the Wanter is in need. You usually appear to be the strong one, so those around you do not know you need help. They cannot see through the bravado—which to you feels like they do not understand you—and after all the caring you have offered them, this can feel like a terrible betrayal. You Wanters know how searing the pain can be when the very people you support cannot read your signals. You have the energy and imagination to know how to take care of others, so why can't they see when you need to be taken care of as well? If you can see what they need, why can't they see what you need?

This dynamic is a torturous one for Wanters. It can feel as if you are invisible, as if everything you have done to reach out to others was never even noticed. Again, even if it was noticed, the assurance you bring when you are caring can fool people into thinking that the reason you do not ask for help is that you do not want any. It is a lonely feeling to know that the yearning you have to make connections—a yearning so strong that it can occupy your entire life experience—is not what others see in you. But for a true Wanter, being seen as one who needs help is even worse. You Wanters are convinced that revealing your needs will ricochet back on you. It is simply not safe. You walk around wanting to be supported, and fearing it as well. This is obviously a no-win situation, and can ultimately wreak havoc on your health.

Wanters and Their Parents: Love with Strings Attached

When most Wanters describe how their parents related to them, they remember that they could not count on their parents' love. As an adult, you may know that your parents loved you, but your experience as a child was that this love was inconsistent and unreliable. Your father was distant, and your mother's affections came with strings attached. You did not experience consistency with either parent, so you learned that love could not be trusted. When asked what you would have liked from your parents, it is the same thing you are now looking for in someone else: to be loved unconditionally.

Wanters and God: Waiting for Proof

You may project onto God the distance that you experienced with your father. Some Wanters look for love in a spiritual practice or community. You wait for God to show you love, or if you are following a certain path, you might wait for enlightenment or fellowship. No matter how you define the Creative Force, you are never convinced by the experiences you have. You are waiting to discover this elusive thing called divinity, or grace, just as you are waiting to experience love. You believe this is in God's hands.

The Wanter's Promise Breaker: Vulnerability

Vulnerability is the Wanter's Promise Breaker. Remember my story in Chapter 4 about Paula, who thought she was a Wanter but could not remember the Promise Breaker? Being vulnerable was a concept so foreign that it was difficult for her to grasp. She had successfully built her life around avoiding vulnerability, so she could hardly conjure up where to begin. It was as if she were being asked to communicate in another language—one with familiar sounds, but she had never used it for her own expression.

You Wanters can probably relate to Paula. You may not even know what vulnerability feels like, though you probably know what it looks like, and you might abhor seeing it in other people. To a Wanter, vulnerability can appear as a weakness or incompetence. In fact, when you Wanters watch as someone who is vulnerable reaps the rewards of love and recognition, you are sometimes absolutely stunned. How could that be? You work hard to meet great challenges and what do you get? Nothing, when compared to people who accomplish a great deal less than you do, yet somehow love comes easily into their lives. It baffles you, as you are so convinced that the way to get anything—including love—is through diligence, strength, and determination. What would it mean if this wasn't true?

There are probably people in your life right now who love you, and you know intellectually that they do, but you still don't feel what you desire. You still want more. Take it from someone who has been there—chances are that it isn't because these people don't love you in the right way. It is probably because you are so armored that you cannot feel their love. And until you create the opening to let it in, you won't ever feel it. Unless you allow yourself to be vulnerable to the very things that you believe are too risky to feel, you are sentencing yourself to the world of wanting.

Vulnerability poses a couple of risks to the Wanter. Obviously, there is the trust factor: Why open yourself up to others when your initial experiences of connection felt so painful? That's an easy one for Wanters to understand. You got hurt, and you are afraid of getting hurt again. But it can't be that simple, since everybody gets hurt, and not everybody resists vulnerability to this degree.

Protect at All Costs

A more complicated risk of vulnerability that is unique to Wanters is your need to protect yourself. You develop a belief that you are the only one you can count on. You are your own best friend. You enjoy your own company, in part because when you are alone, you don't have to put up with the anxiety of being judged unacceptable. You feel safe within yourself, because you are with someone on whom you can rely. And if others do not recognize your achievements, you still know deep down inside that you have done well. In fact, no one can understand you Wanters, or take better care of you, than yourself. When you look around at the ups and downs of relationships, you often shake your head and decide that it makes a lot more sense just to be alone. At least then you know who to trust.

You believe you will lose this nurturing cocoon of the inner self if you become vulnerable. There is an obvious conflict at work here for you Wanters: You say you want love, which suggests intimacy and openness. Then you don't allow yourself to be vulnerable. Instead, you go inside of yourself, where you are safest. You don't know that if you are truly vulnerable, you can experience the same kind of trust and acceptance in relationships that you cling to in the protection of your inner world. And not only will the connection with others provide the welcome staples of reliability and acceptance, it will also bring the recognition, joy, and sense of aliveness that you desire.

If you are a Wanter and imagine living with vulnerability, it may not feel good at first. You may not have any idea of where to start, which in itself can make you feel vulnerable. As a Wanter, you have probably done a lot of amazing things with your life, but I would venture to guess that being truly vulnerable is not one of them. This may be your greatest and most rewarding challenge—and believe me, you will get recognition for this one.

When Safety Is the Issue:
Eleanor's Story

It is important for me to note here that protecting ourselves as children was for some of us not only a matter of feelings but physical safety. In this case, creating vulnerability is a daunting, perhaps impossible, task. I have worked with a number of people who struggle with this ongoing issue in their lives. One of them, Eleanor, is a community organizer who is deeply committed to the causes of social justice, civil rights, and individual empowerment. She is known in a number of political circles as the person to enlist when you need something done right, from putting together an effective rally to successfully managing an election campaign. She has a sharp mind, exudes strength, and is dedicated to her vision for a better world.

Eleanor came to see me when she was in the throes of grieving her father's death. The experience of loss was overwhelming, she explained, as it was the first time she could not rise above her pain and carry on. She wanted to be able to deal with her feelings and move forward. Grief is usually a long-term process of accepting the loss and integrating what many grief counselors call the "the presence of absence" into one's life. It is rarely a matter of dealing with the pain and moving on, but I understood Eleanor's wish to be rid of the feelings, and I trusted that we could work toward acceptance.

Eleanor's father had been a physician who was highly revered in the community, and she had idolized him. Our discussions began with focusing on her loss, but as Eleanor became clear about her covenant, two other areas of concern emerged. They were deeply connected, and both were terribly painful. Eleanor identified her covenant: *As long as I protect others, God will not abandon me.* It was clear to both of us that she lived out this covenant through her political work, which provided a platform for love and recognition.

What was not clear to Eleanor, however, was the persona she exhibited in her role as a protector. She described herself as helping others not only through her organizational savvy, but also by being warm and comforting. I suggested that her political accomplishments, which made a vital difference in expanding opportunities for people, were really the way she expressed her nurturing side. She disagreed, insisting that her "cuddly nature" was what made the difference.

Wanters traditionally express their nurturing side by helping others through work or projects more than through personal contact, but *healthy* Wanters are cognizant of this fact. Eleanor was totally unaware of the incongruity between the way she saw herself and the way the world saw her. She would do almost anything to help others—that was clear—but her manner was more crisp and efficient than cuddly. And even though her words were those of hope and change, she often came across as angry, which was puzzling. Why was she so angry?

This dichotomy was the first issue that emerged. The second had to do with repressed memories. As Eleanor explored her grief, she began to have disturbing recollections, and the more she remembered, the more vivid they became. At first, she just talked about a general feeling of anxiety around her father, but as the weeks went by, she began bringing in details from her past that she had buried for many years. She described her father's huge frame appearing in the doorway of her bedroom night after night, the terror as he lifted her blankets, and the abuse she endured for years.

I have worked with a number of people as they have unearthed childhood traumas, and I have witnessed the excruciating nature of this experience. The challenge for anyone in this situation is to stay true to the feelings that emerge as well as to the possibility of recovery and health. The feelings that surface include rage, guilt, shame, and self-hatred, so it is not easy to consider something as hopeful as recovery when you are in the midst of this kind of an emotional flood.

At this point, for Eleanor to create vulnerability was out of the question. With Eleanor, the purpose of creating a new covenant was to establish the groundwork for healing. This required the ability to be present to the feelings, and this is exactly what Eleanor identified as her next covenant.

Eleanor also had a new perspective on how she related and appeared to others. She understood why she was angry and why so many parts of her were shut down.

Her new covenant is *When I am aware of my vulnerability, I am in a full relationship with God.* The covenant does not ask her to be vulnerable, but it does suggest that by being aware of her vulnerability, she is closer to God. Eleanor thought this captured her situation well, as she felt her many years of denial kept her from truly experiencing her connection with God. It was not until she could accept her own pain that she could also feel she had a relationship with her Higher Power.

How Wanters Look for Love: "See Me, Love Me"

Wanters look for love through recognition. You look for someone to understand you, as you feel that this is the way you will feel the love that you never received as a child. You Wanters cannot truly feel love, no matter how much recognition you get, until you face your own vulnerability. But you don't realize this, so when you don't feel loved, you blame the other person. You cannot fathom that the ability to feel loved is your responsibility. You do not consider it your job to make sure you are open to the feelings you are looking for. When it comes to love, you Wanters are stuck in a chicken and egg kind of dilemma. You cannot risk the vulnerability to see your role in the dynamic, but you will not feel vulnerable enough to experience love until you understand this principle.

You Wanters may consider yourselves overly responsible, and in many areas of your life you are. You are most likely responsible for accomplishing great successes, which is to be commended. But the more subtle responsibility is the one in which you own your behaviors and the impact they have on yourself and others. For you Wanters, this is the case not only in intimate relationships, but also in your daily interactions.

"Why Do I Have to Change If It's Their Problem?"

You Wanters don't always realize it, but you can easily cross the border between being impressive and intimidating. In your pursuit of recognition, you have created an interesting life, and you come across as an impressive individual. When you enter a room, you are immediately noticed for your boundless energy and enthusiasm. The internal pain and disappointment I have talked about in this chapter are lucid for you, but at the same time you appear strong and happy-go-lucky. You may enter into a casual conversation and soon find yourself dominating the discussion because in your mind the other person has not spoken up. If the other person had something to say, he or she would say it. Or you may hear feedback from a colleague about an interaction that left someone feeling as if he or she had been bullied, but when you think back over the same incident you remember an innocent, playful argument. You wonder what was wrong with the other person.

If you have been on the fence about whether this style fits you, let me pose a question: Do you usually conclude that the other person is the one who needs to speak up? Do you ever find yourself saying, "Why do I have to change the way I am to make it easier for other people to be around me? Why isn't it their responsibility to take care of themselves?" Or, "It isn't my fault if other people feel intimidated around me. I am not going to make myself smaller for their sake."

Advice from a Wanter

If the previous questions resonate for you, here are some insights I have picked up through my own healing as a Wanter that you might want to consider for yourself. When we are perceived as dominating a conversation, there is a good chance that we *are* dominating the conversation. This is in part because of the other people, of course. Yes, it would be great if they could speak up and let us know how they feel. But we are also in the conversation. Can't we see our role? And if we can see it, why don't we change what we are doing so that we have a more positive impact? What would happen if we actually read the cues and responded in a way that improved the dynamic?

In terms of others wanting us to be "small"—or whatever the word is for you—my personal work on this issue has suggested that other people don't want us to be small. They want us to be real. They want us to let go of the bravado we have constructed and just be ourselves. They want to connect on an even playing field, and they cannot figure out how.

At this point you might say, "If they cared, they would know how." I have been down this road on my own journey, so let me ask you—How would they know? It is up to us to create the possibility for connection. We cannot expect people to know what we want. We must reveal ourselves honestly. When we intimidate others, we are most likely showing them our protected side. It is not their job to see through this protection. It is our job to own the fact that we protect ourselves, acknowledge how this influences ourselves and others, and then choose whether we want to run our lives this way. And if we choose not to, we need to learn to be responsible, which in this case requires us to be vulnerable.

Vulnerability Begets Love

When you Wanters embrace vulnerability, you are able to see the difference between love and recognition. You can develop deep loving relationships separately from gaining recognition. Vulnerability also allows you to forgive others, including those from the past who may have contributed to your earliest wounds so that you are no longer seeking to fill a void that began in your childhood.

Vulnerability allows you to forgive yourself as well. In the process of healing your covenants, you Wanters sometimes discover that you made sense of what you perceived to be a lack of love in your family by deciding you were bad or not lovable. It is important to note that even if your family was close, you may have felt you did not get the nurturing you needed. The power of the covenant is the same whether it is based on perception or reality. You must reconcile with your childhood so that you can move forward with your life.

Who Is Left to Take Responsibility?

When you make room in your life for forgiveness, you don't have much room left for blame. And if you are not blaming others, who is left to take responsibility?

When I pose this question to Wanters, they honestly do not

know. When I suggest that they take responsibility for accepting their role in relationships, they are often mystified. Some of them stare back at me as if this were the first time they have heard the concept. For some of them, it is the first time they have "heard" it, as they have brought themselves to my office with a willingness to change, so they are open to hearing possibilities.

You must take responsibility to create the vulnerability required to feel the love you want. When you do, you will be surprised by the results. Vulnerability begets love. When you take responsibility for creating love instead of waiting for it to come to you via recognition—or the right person—you liberate yourself from the illusion that you are dependent on others for your intimacy. Once you take the risk to be seen as the lovable person you know you are, it is as if you were suddenly living in color after years of black and white.

This can be a long road, but the journey is well worth it. Once you Wanters take responsibility for relationships, you are then free to create connections however you want them. You are not relying on others to treat you in a particular way. Once you reach this realization, you begin to truly love. After years of managing connections in order to fill old longings, you now create love for love's sake.

The result of this change is awe-inspiring. As you begin to connect with others from their own authentic place, the love that comes back opens your heart. What was once a Promise Breaker—to be vulnerable with others—now allows you to have exactly what you have been wanting.

The Wanter's Life Prayer: The Sacred Checklist

You who confuse love with recognition have mastered the art of drawing attention to yourself. One of the most effective ways to create this recognition—and to feel love—is through excellence and accomplishment. In order to keep yourself looking like achievers, you Wanters keep your mind on what it takes to get the job done. The moment you open your eyes, you know what is on the list for that day. You know how to proceed to meet your goals. You wake up thinking about vision, tasks, and strategies, and all for the sake of creating the recognition that you believe is a form of love.

How Wanters Define Success: The Success of the Successful

Wanters enjoy success. In the workplace, you often get into a project on the ground floor, guide it through its ups and downs, and then stand back as it comes into a form all its own. Whatever system or organization you are in, the results of your work have your name on them, and that is important to you. Things come out differently when you run the show. You have a touch for bringing people and plans together in such a way that your vision is reached and you have a satisfying experience along the way. You Wanters make good managers, but you make better directors, chief executive officers, and entrepreneurs. Wanters do the best job possible, and when it is successful—which it usually is—you know you are often the primary reason why. It really feels great when you are recognized for a job well done.

If Your Partner Is a Wanter: Support Your Partner to Let the Love In

Those of you who are involved with Wanters have your work cut out for you. Wanters need their friends and loved ones to give them the freedom to be vulnerable. They need an environment in which they can let down the masterminded persona of their incredible, flawless self and allow their whole being—both the good and the bad, the weak and the strong, the amazing and the mundane—to be accepted. Wanters need a partner who will bear witness to their weaknesses without turning away.

Remember that Wanters are unable to discern between love and recognition. Thus, when they need your help (which they experience as a hybrid of love), they perform in a way that catches your eye. For example, when they ask for your support, they say it in the language of the Wanter: They do more. They work more, accomplish more, go the extra mile.

Wanters can also become demanding when they need support, but unfortunately their demands are channeled in the wrong direction. They might insist that *you* have a problem, and *you* need to change. If you are involved with someone who is dominated by the Wanter style, you will be expected to translate this into a call for help. This may sound manipulative, and at first glance, it is. But when Wanters are out of balance, they are not able to have their needs met in a straightforward way. Of course, the responsible thing for them to do would be to ask for help. But unless they resolve their law-based covenant, they simply are not equipped to make that choice.

I can remember how exasperated people were with me when I could not make myself vulnerable. Now I see that until I changed my covenant, I was restricted, in my own mind, from making those choices. I am not saying this to excuse myself or other Wanters, but to shed light on what can appear to be manipulation.

As with Givers, there will be times when the Wanter's inability to ask for help can mean a life-or-death difference. Wanters have to face their mistrust of others, as that is the only way they will be able to receive help. The key for those of you who are involved with Wanters is to demonstrate, again and again, that when a little sliver of frailty is exposed, you still care for them, their neediness does not overwhelm you, and the possibility that they have weak spots is acceptable. In fact, it is worth celebrating.

When the Wanter Creates a Faith-Based Covenant

Once you create a faith-based covenant, you can begin to balance your strength and drive with softness. You can understand how the job of experiencing love is in your court—and, being Wanters, you want to do a good job, so you learn to take responsibility for your feelings. This frees you from the no-win situation of blaming your partner when you are not finding the love you seek, and allows you to focus on what it is in your own life that needs to heal.

CHAPTER 7

The Promise of the Searcher

If we find nothing of interest where we are, we are likely
to find little of lasting interest where we wish to go.

—*Edwin Way Teale*

Some of the most delightful people I know are Searchers. These
are the people with the most entertaining stories about the places
they've traveled, the latest personal growth workshop they've
attended, or the new job they are starting, because the last one
turned out to be a bore. Of course, most of us are Searchers for
a while in life, and there is a healthy streak to that adventurous
spirit that none of us want to lose—but there is also a downside
to constantly looking, looking, looking.

Searchers believe they must keep going around the bend for the next good thing. There is always something more to be found, something better. This is why some of my clients walk out my office door to find the next therapeutic model to help them. Searchers believe that God will love them as long as they

- Keep moving

- Don't miss out on the next exciting thing

- Find the right path

- Explore all of life's opportunities

- Don't settle for less

- Make a change

If you are a Searcher, you know the cycle: You seek out something, someone, or some answer, and you almost always find it. For a while, life is looking up. You feel filled with the promise of a brand-new day. And then something changes. If it's the perfect job you have found, your co-workers might begin to annoy you, or you don't agree with your boss's politics, or it looks to you as if the office isn't running as smoothly as possible. For some of us, these are just bumps in the road that we learn to live with. But if you are a Searcher, chances are that you take these impressions as signals that it is time to move on.

You Searchers will often focus your pursuit of the next new thing on finding a spiritual path. Many Searchers have passed through my office on their way to or from a spiritual journey. If you are a Searcher, this may sound familiar: You set your sights on the feeling of peace and sense of belonging that faith and community have to offer, and you usually find them. But you also discover that a regime of meditation or prayer may be required, and that being in a community not only involves joy and companionship, but also rules, limitations, and sometimes being with people you just don't like. When you realize that you have landed yourself in a place that requires disciplined behavior and the ability to tolerate others, you see it as a sign that it is time to move on.

Ongoing life changes are your only option because you are unable to make a commitment to a deeper purpose in your life. And because you cannot make the choice to focus on one thing—Searchers are constantly driven, always revved up with the engines in gear—your searching is not within your power. You do not have control over your impulse to be on the move. When it feels like it is time to go, you are gone. It is as if you have no choice. If others want to discuss it with you or suggest other alternatives, you are not able to be flexible. And that is exactly why pure, unbalanced Searching is not healthy—because health requires flexibility and balance.

The Queen of Possibilities: Wendy's Story

Wendy is a Searcher who came to me several years ago, and still sends me e-mails—at first from Miami, now from Austin. Wendy calls herself the Queen of Possibilities. She is creative and talented, and she simply cannot miss out on anything. Her covenant is *As long I keep sampling everything, God will love me*.

Wendy has held a number of professional positions, all of them interesting, but she continually moves from one to another, explaining that the next opportunity is the one that will really work. Wendy has been transferring to the job that will really work for so long that her track record is becoming a liability. This was the issue that brought her to me in the first place, as some of her colleagues warned her against a job switch she was considering (and ultimately took), because they felt she needed a stable position in her field if she wanted to further her career.

Wendy dabbled in finding a new covenant. She told herself that she needed to build a professional foundation based on her accomplishments rather than creating a vision based on her dreams. She told me she knew her workplace experiences were valuable, but having the right degree was also critical. She knew she should stay in one place long enough to acquire some of the credentials that others in her field had already earned. She had started to develop a new covenant along the lines of *As long as I have a foundation that supports my changes, I will be in a true relationship with my Higher Power.* Before we got to the place where Wendy could commit to it, however, she decided to take the new job—it was just too interesting to turn down, she explained when she called to cancel our last appointment—and was gone.

One of the important things to acknowledge with clients such as Wendy is that they are not necessarily motivated by the destinations to which they are always heading, nor are they responding to a true calling with every new journey. If they were, I counsel these clients, they would be able to make the choice to either stay in one place or to pursue a new horizon. But searching controls their entire lives. It dominates their decisions about relationships, work, and home. The saddest thing is that Searching is not an authentic muse. It is only a behavior they have acquired—just like giving or wanting—because of their law-based covenants. Searchers continually make changes because they are unable to find meaning and purpose in one thing.

Though it can look to others as if Searchers are lazy or just can't buckle down, it is not that simple. If you are a Searcher, you are probably a hard worker. As you well know, it is not an easy task to keep moving and changing, and to keep coming up with new things to try. You Searchers are often creative, artistic individuals. You listen to your inner musings. You follow your dreams, but you cannot always stick around to realize them, and that's when dreams really come true.

Searchers and Stress: "Gotta Go!"

To the Searcher, stress is a huge exit sign. If you are a Searcher, chances are that stress makes you feel absolutely helpless. You do not have the inner resolve to take on the problem yourself, and you do not have the confidence to assume there may be someone else out there to fix it. It is just too hard, and you have to leave.

If you are a Searcher, this can be a difficult thing to admit. You may feel as if you are a coward, as if you should be able to face whatever troubles come your way and deal with them. You may feel ashamed to admit it, but you may remember a number of times when things just got too hard and you headed for the door. Or you may not even know that you had a choice to stay in the situation and develop a response to whatever was stressful. Many of you are truly unaware of the possibility that you can stay in a difficult situation and see it through. In your mind, why should you?

To you Searchers who choose to move on when stress gets overwhelming, here's a heads-up: Sooner or later, you will be faced with a life crisis and there will be no way out. You will not be able to leave. If you become sick, for example, you obviously cannot get up and march out of the hospital.

I must say, though, that when I work with Searchers who are diagnosed with serious illnesses, I am impressed with their uncanny ability to continue searching. Despite the IV tubes and monitors that appear to tether them to their beds, they often leave anyway—but now, their searching is done through their fantasies. Sometimes I see Searchers do this through romanticizing the experience of being sick. It becomes a drama, a piece of theater in which they just happen to be cast. Or they jump from one promise of healing to another, convinced that if they just find the right intervention, they will be cured.

In fact, drifting into an imaginary world when you are dealing with serious illness is not necessarily unhealthy. It can be an excellent way to cope for a while, and my patients who are Givers and Wanters could benefit from this practice.

The advice I bring to Searchers in this situation is that it is great to escape every so often, but you also need to focus on your healing as it is right here, in this bed, in this moment. You need to commit not just to your comfort—as escape offers great relief—but to the larger picture of recovery. But focusing on the bigger picture requires the kind of inner belief and commitment of purpose with which a Searcher has difficulty.

Searchers and Blame: "Don't Ask Me"

Givers blame themselves, and Wanters blame other people, but the Searcher really does not know who to blame. It is just too confusing, and you do not want to be forced to decide. Searchers are often tempted to wonder if whatever is going on is just a message from the universe—and it may be—but this conclusion does not help you to focus on how to overcome the crisis.

For Searchers, blame is about commitment: deciding who to blame and actually following through by saying it entails taking a stand for something. If you make the choice to blame someone—whether yourself or another person—you have got to have the conviction that you are right. And to have this, you need the inner strength it takes to believe that you *can* be right. If you are a Searcher, you most likely observe how other people have faith in themselves, or you watch them come up with an unshakable confidence to do whatever it takes, and you believe that this is simply out of your league. You cannot imagine what it would be like to take a stand for something and believe in it, especially if it is about finding blame or fault in someone else.

How Searchers Ask for Help: "No Problem!"

Here is a place where Searchers differ enormously from Givers and Wanters. If you are a Searcher, you have absolutely no problem asking for help. It never occurs to you, as it does to the Givers or the Wanters, that needing help is a sign of something to be avoided, such as weakness, because the truth of the matter is that you accept what others consider to be weakness. The challenge for you is not to ask for help, but to stick with the advice or assistance when you find it.

One thing that can make a real difference is to have someone in your life who is a role model or a mentor. Having someone close to you who has the strength you cannot find within yourself allows you to experiment with what it might be like to be strong on your own. Mentors cannot duplicate the inner foundation that Searchers need—you must get in touch with your own—but as you receive ongoing support, the Searcher can begin to feel what it is like to be grounded. This is especially true when the mentor is involved in whatever new venture you have begun. If you can find someone to guide you and help keep you focused, you may have a better chance of developing the deeper commitment you need.

Searchers and Their Parents: The Searching Childhood

You Searchers may remember that your father was unable to commit in his own life. He may have been perceived as weak in the eyes of the world, and was most comfortable with his children when they, too, were underachievers. As a Searcher, you felt most loved when you appeared to be fragile. Demonstrating strength in any way meant risking your father's love and approval.

Your mother may have been loving, but when you wanted to feel her nurturing, you learned early on that the best way to do this was to be sick, or to appear to be needy. Then she would shower you with care and affection. With both parents, Searchers learned that love was conditional. In a child's way of seeing the world, the way to get your parents' attention was to maintain the appearance of being a little tired, confused, and afraid. It was as if you believed that your youthful courage could add insult to the injury that you knew, deep down, your parents experienced in life.

Many of the Searchers I have worked with have discovered that they kept themselves at half-mast when they were children, because they felt that by revealing themselves as strong they might expose their parents as weak. Though they could intuit this, it was of course too overwhelming, so they created a covenant to make sense of their world. The covenant keeps them moving and changing, because staying in one place requires commitment.

If your parents were Searchers, they probably did not encourage you to excel in any particular area, or to find your calling. If you are a Searcher, you may not have had the childhood experience of focusing on one thing, such as baseball or music, and trying to do your best at one pursuit. Instead, you may remember wandering from one interest to another, but never becoming engaged enough to enjoy success. This can be a lonely and unsatisfying experience for a child.

The Hurried Wanderer:
Wayne's Story

One of my clients once told me that his parents always said, "When things get tough, keep moving." Wayne remembered his parents as being loving and kind, but not successful in the material sense. His parents each had a limited education, and they never encouraged their children to follow through on school projects. They certainly never mentioned college. And because they each worked, sometimes holding down two jobs, things could get a little chaotic in Wayne's house. "I became a hurried person," he told me.

Wayne left home after high school and began to drift through a series of low-paying jobs, never staying at one long enough to earn a raise or be promoted. He was an amiable guy and got along well with others, so his employers wanted him to stay, but he just couldn't do it.

Wayne's covenant was *As long as I keep moving, God will make life easy for me*, and that was precisely what he did. Wayne knew he appeared to be a failure, but he also knew within himself that he had more potential. His neighborhood was full of families like his own who struggled financially, and now that he was out in the world, he saw opportunities to be more successful. He knew this required sticking to something, but every time he tried and every time he encountered conflict or frustration, he defaulted to his covenant. The only option he would allow himself to consider was to move on.

Wayne and I talked about what it would mean if he committed his Promise Breaker and actually stuck with one job, and he realized that it would mean he would "show up his parents." His failures, he realized, were his way of protecting his parents, as if his success would be hurtful to them. Eventually he realized that even if it was hurtful to them—in fact, they were very proud as he began to establish himself—he had to take the risk. Wayne told me he wanted to slow down, stay in one place, and give himself the chance to shine, no matter what. His faith-based covenant is *As long as I can stand still and reflect on my life, I will be more fully in a relationship with God*.

The last time I saw Wayne, he had been at one job for

almost six months—a record for him. It wasn't easy and he often wanted to leave, but each time he got the impulse to walk out he remembered to stand still. So far, it was giving him what he wanted.

Searchers and God: Searching for God in All the Right Places

You Searchers know that you are continually looking for the right kind of God to relate to. Because you did not enter into adulthood with the tools needed to create commitment, you have never made peace with one path. Your relationship with God never really starts or ends—you are simply moving from one idea about spirituality to the next.

The Searcher's Promise Breaker: Commitment

In a way, the Searcher glorifies the true American explorer, and this style is often romanticized by the media. The independent-minded artist, the spiritual seeker, and the lone cowboy are all model images for the Searcher. In fact, we live in a nation founded by searchers, as the colonists and settlers were all seeking a new life (at the expense of those who'd been living here for centuries, I must add). Historically, we live in a place called the New World.

Here's the irony: Artists need to express themselves and to find their voice. But unless they include form to their painting, technique to their dance, or structure to their writing, they are limited in their expression. Unless spiritual seekers stick to a practice, they will eventually veer from the path. And though it might appear as if the lone cowboy is wandering on horseback all day, he is actually herding cattle across vast plains and must focus on the route, the weather, and timing—or risk losing everything.

Commitment is the Searcher's Promise Breaker. If you are a Searcher, commitment may appear to sabotage the muse. It means losing out on the next exciting thing, or staying on this side of the fence and missing the grass that is so much greener on the other side. For many people, commitment poses no question: When we want something, we stay committed through the ups and downs, as much as possible, until we get it. But if you are a Searcher, commitment appears to be the thing that restricts you. It threatens your freedom. It might keep you from wandering off into the possibility of doing something else, and you are not willing to give that up.

If you are a Searcher and the people at your new job are no longer fun to be around, or you start to feel bored around someone who just last week felt like the love of your life, it may never even occur to you to question your commitment. You can't question it because you simply do not know that you have any. Just like the Giver's own voice is silent and the Wanter is oblivious to his or her vulnerability, you Searchers are completely unaware of your ability to follow through with whatever challenge is in front of you.

Many of us could use a little more diligence when it comes to knuckling down and keeping ourselves on the project before us, but this is different. For a Searcher, making a commitment is not just about seeing something through to complete a task. For you, it is about eliminating the distraction that constant movement and change can provide. Because even when your search appears to be fueled by spiritual longing, what you really need to do is commit to one purpose in life. For you, commitment is the path to peace.

You Searchers have a good reason for not committing. You learned in your childhood that if you committed to anything, your strength could scare away your parents' love. Success is not what brings a Searcher love—in fact, you were raised to believe that success could drive it off. There is another aspect to commitment that keeps you on the move as well: It hurts. Not because it is difficult— I know that Searchers do a lot of difficult things.

The pain in commitment is internal. When you slow down to focus on one thing, you create the space and time to hear your own inner voice. If you are a Searcher, you know that this can be intolerable. Whatever pain and sorrow you might have stored up inside is muffled by the sound of change.

Givers must have their voices heard, and Wanters must take responsibility for themselves in relationships. In the same vein, you Searchers must come face-to-face with whatever is inside of you that you fear will show up if you stop in one place.

"As Long as I Keep Moving": Luis's Story

Fear of commitment was clearly the situation with Luis, whose father was absent and whose mother was often ill. When I met Luis, he was in his early 30s, working one job, married, and the father of a newborn. He described his past 10 years as a jumble of different adventures, workplaces, and relationships. They were all fairly satisfying, but now he wanted to stay committed to one thing, since he had a family. Within two months of our first meeting, he decided to move to Stockholm; his wife was Swedish and wanted to live closer to her family. He said he would be able to create work through contacts he knew in Spain. Luis was also working on an advanced degree, so he anticipated coming back to the United States every few months to meet with his advisors.

By becoming an absentee graduate student, Luis risked dropping out. One of the biggest challenges Searchers face is the ability to follow through and finish what they have begun, and living halfway around the world from his professors and classmates would not support Luis to complete the program. I asked him about this, suggesting that he design his life in such a way that when they got to Sweden he could stay in one place in order to complete his degree and secure a local job. Luis discussed this possibility, but I could tell he was drifting as we spoke. I felt that though we were in my office in San Francisco, Luis's thoughts were already partially in Stockholm and partially in Madrid.

Luis moved to Sweden, and he took the job in Spain. Despite my doubt, he earned his degree, and I am glad I was wrong about that one. For a while, Luis and I kept in touch through e-mail, and he told me that living in Stockholm was stressful. The last time I heard from him, he was considering living in Spain full-time, which would mean leaving his marriage. He loved his family, but he found the difficulties of moving to a new city and sharing his wife with her family to be intolerable. He told me he was desperately torn. "Living here is so hard," he wrote in one of his last messages, "that I feel like it has stopped me in my tracks."

This was a telling line. Luis's original covenant was *As long as I keep on moving, God will keep me safe.* He never made a new one when we were working together—he was out the door too fast. I do not know where he is now, as his e-mails ended and my messages were returned when I tried to reach him. I hope he knows that he can be safe, whether he is moving or not.

Was Luis irresponsible? In some ways, of course, yes. He is accountable for his behavior, but that does not mean he is able to change it without some serious personal work. Just as the Wanter's inability to be vulnerable and the Giver's difficulty with speaking up are extensions of their covenants, Luis was defaulting to his. Luis simply could not endure the pain that can be part of a lifelong commitment.

What happens if you are a Searcher and you commit to something? Once you slow down, you feel trapped. You feel cornered, face-to-face with your feelings. Searching is a dependable escape hatch, and now that door is closed. When you decide to pursue one thing, you are no longer focused on running. And once that happens, you must take responsibility for whatever it is that you are running from.

This is where the pain comes in. For a Searcher, commitment looks like doors are closing, but in fact, it actually creates opportunity. If you are a Searcher, learning to commit can turn your life around. Sometimes it doesn't even matter what you commit to, just as long as you can thoroughly experience what it feels like to actually focus and follow through on one thing.

God Helps Those Who Search: Shirley's Story

Another one of my clients, Shirley, was able to make the leap from searching to commitment. She was used to moving from job to job in the human services field. She wanted to "help those who were down," she told me, but she was not a Giver; the covenant that ruled her life was *As long as I keep looking, God will help me keep it together.* Shirley lost her parents at a young age. She lived with different relatives, all of whom she described as very nice, but it was clear that she carried the grief from her childhood loss. This experience drew her to human services, but every time she became close to her co-workers, she changed jobs. She thought she could not find the job that was right for her, but as we talked I wondered if the fear of confronting her loss kept her looking for a new position.

Shirley wanted to shift out of the hands-on aspect of her work and get involved in policy analysis, but she knew she had to go back to school in order to do so. Shirley was excited about following her dream, but she told me that the possibility of going to school, which required several years of being in one place, felt like suffocation. As we worked together, we focused on two things: first, her loss as well as the painful years of being shuttled between several families, and second, her interest in this particular kind of work. The more we talked, the more she was able to reduce the fear and sorrow she carried with her and to increase her vision of herself professionally. Eventually, she created this covenant *When I am committed to myself and my work, I am in a more authentic relationship with God.*

Shirley has remained in contact over the years. She sends cards from Sacramento, where she works on state policies in human services.

How Searchers Look for Love: Somewhere Over the Rainbow

For you Searchers, love is an ongoing quest. The experience of new love is easy for you to find, as you are ripe for the rapture of infatuation, but the commitment that is required to deepen love, or to keep it alive, often eludes you entirely. As we all know, one of the things that a long-term relationship needs is not the romance and Eros of new love—it is the ability to plan for the future.

You Searchers do not plan. In a relationship, planning asks for a context in which the relationship resides. It requires you to decide what meaning the partnership has in your life, and you Searchers resist looking at the larger meaning of anything because it requires taking a stand. In my work with couples, I have seen a number of Searchers who genuinely feel love for their partners, but lose the relationship because they simply cannot plan for the future. If you are a Searcher, you probably like to wing it. If you cannot, you usually move on.

The Searcher's Life Prayer: The Next Journey

If you are a Searcher, you might greet the day with a new adventure. You might turn over a new leaf, or resolve to begin again, because it is by starting anew that your law-based covenant is kept alive. You need to keep looking, and in order to stay on the move, you need to make a fresh start every day. You are tireless in your enthusiasm for possibilities.

Searchers and Success: Start Your Engines

It's a new morning. There is a new plan about to be hatched: It's the first day of a new job, or your new lover just called, or the tickets for the next trip feel crisp in your hands. If you are a Searcher, these kinds of things feel successful. Beginnings, without the tedium of familiarity. You are starting something new yet again, and this is what you do best.

If Your Partner Is a Searcher

Searchers are charming and inventive, and their roller-coaster lives are a lot of fun. For anyone looking for a great ride, Searchers are the perfect mate. But if you are looking for a partner who will stick by you no matter what, why have you chosen a Searcher? No matter how much you impress a Searcher—with your looks, your wit, your sexy energy—none of this can compete with leaving.

The last two decades have ushered in a new genre of relationship books. Many of them advise readers to question why they choose certain partner types, especially if they are not happy with them. If you are involved with a Searcher, and if the Searcher is not showing signs of committing to anything in his or her life, this may be a good time to ask yourself the same question.

Searchers who live with a responsible form of wanderlust are a different matter. These Searchers have enjoyed their journeys and are now able to have the real adventure: commitment. Because they are Searchers, however, they will get distracted now and then, but once Searchers are ready to commit, they respond well to loving support that keeps them on track. Just keep reminding your partner of where he or she wants to be.

When a Searcher Creates a Faith-Based Covenant

When you develop a faith-based covenant that supports commitment, it may look as if the content of the commitment is where the difficulty resides. If it is a job, the work itself may seem challenging—a lot of work is. If it is a relationship, the partner may introduce all sorts of issues—but most people do. It is important for you to face the feelings that are within you as you engage in commitment. These feelings are connected to a conditional law-based covenant. That is the root of the pain, and for the Searcher, it is also the source of healing.

CHAPTER 8

Identifying Your Interior, Exterior, and Quiet Covenant Styles

What lies behind us, and what lies before us are tiny matters, compared to what lies within us."

—*Ralph Waldo Emerson*

We need to find one covenant style among the three to identify as our own in order to change our covenant, but I know that many of us often identify with two styles. Most of the participants at my workshops and the clients I see in counseling report that they may see themselves appearing as one of the Giver, Wanter, or Searcher styles, but on the inside they feel as if they are another. If you find the same thing to be true for yourself, you are on to something important in terms of creating a faith-based covenant.

EXERCISE 6

Determine Your Three Different Styles

We have been over a lot of material since you put your journals away. It is now time to bring them out again to help understand the different ways in which we use the styles in our lives. Open to a fresh page and allow yourself as much time as you need to respond to the following questions:

1. Where do you feel most free to be yourself? You might think that everyone feels most free in their own home, but the truth is that some of us are able to let our guard down more at work, or when we are by ourselves.

2. What makes it easy in this situation to be yourself? When you imagine where you are when you feel free to be yourself, reflect on what the situation offers that contributes to your sense of ease as well as what goes on inside you. Why is this situation different from others?

3. Where do you feel that you cannot be yourself? When we truly ask ourselves this question, some of us realize that we are not as able to be ourselves with friends, family, or our significant other as we thought we could be. If you have this feeling, or are surprised in any way by your response, take a moment to sit with this feeling.

4. What is it about this situation that makes it difficult to be yourself? Even if your answer to the preceding question was one you expected—you cannot be yourself in the office, for example, or in the company of your spouse's friends— take some time to look at why you allowed that situation to keep you separated from who you really are.

5. Do you feel more comfortable in a group, with a significant other, or alone? This inquiry may be trickier than it

appears. Many of us have learned to manage being in crowds, or we have figured out how to spend time alone, but we may not feel comfortable. Spend a moment to think beyond the situations you are capable of being in, and consider instead the ones you truly prefer.

6. When you are in a group, which of your behaviors are valued? Which behaviors are not valued? Exploring these questions may help you to understand how much you manage yourself in a group and how much you allow yourself just to be. For some of us, if we do not trust that we are valued for who we are, we find specific behaviors that we feel are acceptable and present those when we are with others.

7. Are there behaviors you want to bring to a relationship or a group that you feel may not be accepted? If so, think about where you allow yourself to express these behaviors.

8. Are there behaviors you see in other people that you wonder about having in your own life, and if so, what keeps you from choosing them? What would happen if you allowed yourself to experience these behaviors? These questions can offer further insights into your covenant, as it may reinforce the ideas you already have about what you need to integrate into your life to live in balance. Whatever you need to create balance will be included in your faith-based covenant.

Different Styles in the Same Person

Each of us has an interior style and an exterior style. Knowing which style is interior and which is exterior is crucial:

- Your interior style is based on your spiritual agreement and is often where your true feelings reside, including the feelings you do not want to see. Knowing your interior style will help you understand your law-based covenant and your Promise Breaker.

- Your exterior style is one you have created to conform to the demands of society, the workplace, or relationships. If you focus on your exterior style, you may gain insights about your behaviors, but you will not be able to create the most supportive faith-based covenant for yourself.

The challenge is not to choose the one we like the most or the one we want to be, but to identify the style that is truly our own and to allow it to mix freely with the other two, creating a balance of all three styles. Until we heal our covenants and live with more balance, most of us will blend two styles. I will go into this subject in more detail later, but here is a snapshot of what the blends might look like:

- *Interior Givers, Exterior Searchers:* Interior Givers may realize that they are exterior Searchers, because the image of the seeker serves to keep them from using their own voice.

- *Interior Wanters, Exterior Givers:* True Wanters may have learned to portray the characteristics of Givers, as they are more acceptable. They often manage their fear of rejection by appearing as if they were giving and caring instead of honoring the true natures of their energetic drives.

- *Interior Searchers, Exterior Givers or Wanters:* True Searchers may have adapted to some situations as a Giver and to others as a Wanter. This is endemic to the style, as Searchers are looking for an external persona to bring to the world.

These are not the only combinations, and no style is better or worse than another. It is important to remember that the goal of creating a faith-based covenant is not to "fix" our interior or our exterior styles, but instead to empower the healthiest aspects of

all parts of ourselves. This gives us access to the positive qualities of all three styles. When we can move seamlessly from one
style to another in a conscious relationship with our Higher
Power, we realize the promise of our soul.

The Quiet Style

If most of us negotiate our lives with two out of the three styles,
what happens to the third style? For many of us, the third style
is almost forgotten. I call it our quiet style, and understanding its
role in our lives can be very important. When we gain access to
all three styles, the quiet style emerges as a fresh perspective,
which truly adds balance and health to our lives.

In a way, the quiet style can sound like a Promise Breaker, as
it is a part of ourselves we have kept out of the spotlight. Unlike
our Promise Breaker, however, the quiet style is not forbidden to
us. In fact, it is often something we yearn to have in our lives, but
do not permit ourselves. For many of us, the quiet style is our creative, imaginative side. It is the inner peace we remember having when we used to write in our journals, or when we would
bring a sketchbook outside and draw whatever caught our eye.
How long has it been since you felt this peace?

For some of us, the quiet style may now be tempered within
ourselves, but when we allow it to coexist with our other two
styles it will not seem quiet at all. That's because for some of us
the style we keep quiet manifests the forceful, driven part of ourselves. Once we develop our faith-based agreement and feel the
support of God in pursuing balance in our lives, we no longer
need to suppress our drive. We can allow it to take shape in its
true form, whatever that means for us.

For some of us, the quiet style is not about creativity or power.
Instead, it is the part of us that aches to reach out in a nurturing,
supportive way, but we have kept this under wraps, as if it were

not acceptable for us. We may have watched as others followed their natural impulse to nurture and care, and we may have longed to do the same thing, but somehow we just couldn't allow ourselves to. In this case, when we are able to honor our desires to be tender and loving, we are living in balance with our quiet style.

Faith-Based Covenants and Our Styles

Our new faith-based spiritual agreements allow us to

1. Own and empower the positive qualities of our interior style so that we can live from it with full awareness, rather than defaulting to it blindly

2. Integrate the strengths of the exterior style, taking advantage of the skills we have acquired through adapting our behavior to outside influences

3. Embrace the quiet style, exploring behaviors that may never have occurred to us to try.

Before I created my faith-based covenant, I was a blend of an interior Wanter and an exterior Giver, so my quiet style was the Searcher. When I was able to identify my agreement and understand the other styles, I recognized my attempts at appearing as if I were a Giver. I felt I was supportive and nurturing with my colleagues, and, as is the case with many Wanters, I knew that the spirit of my work was as caring as anyone else's skills in giving. But, at the same time, I wanted to appear as if I were doing good in the way that most Givers do. I was not aware of it at the time, but now I can see that I felt giving would be more acceptable than my energetic drive for understanding. Appearing as if I were a Giver might also overshadow my strength and power, about which I was ambivalent. And if I behaved like a Giver, I might have a better chance of earning the recognition I craved.

The trouble was that I was simply not an effective Giver. I could make the gestures, and I usually brought a spirit of generosity to most interactions, but my focus was more on getting a job done than it was on nurturing others. Once I identified my covenant and was able to accept my vulnerability, I could choose to soften the driving impulse behind my Wanter style. Then integrating the skills of a Giver was not an either-or decision. I was able to access all three styles without feeling I was violating my covenant to do so.

I discovered my quiet style as well. It is playful and childlike. I experience it as often as I can now. An example of an incident when I was first getting comfortable with it sticks out in my mind. I was at a family camp with Ruth and our two sons. We attended the camp every year through our church, so I knew a lot of the people. I had established a particular reputation. I was one of the guys who led the spiritual service sometimes, and often organized the events.

It rained every single day this particular week. By the end of the week, the kids were going stir-crazy—even Ping-Pong has its limits—and the adults were weary of sitting around the mess hall, drinking coffee and talking. One of my friends decided to take over. He gathered up a bunch of the kids and adults and led us to the top of a grassy hill, where we stood in the pouring rain waiting for what he had planned. Then he stripped off his shirt, belly-flopped onto the mud, and went careening down on his front, shouting with joy as the mud covered him. The kids followed him right away, and soon many of the adults were sliding down to the huge puddle at the bottom and shrieking with laughter when they hit the chilly water.

In the past, I would have stayed on the hilltop, enjoying the chaos but never joining in. The degree of playfulness would have made me appear too vulnerable. But now, I didn't care. I was no longer committed to keeping myself safe and in control. I could throw caution to the wind and go for it, which is usually what a Searcher would do. I threw my shirt on the ground and dove down the hill, "yahooing" at the top of my lungs. And then I ran back up, exhilarated, and did it again and again, all afternoon. By the end of the day, I was dirty, wet, hoarse, and happy.

This does not sound like much of a "quiet" style, of course. I am intentionally using this example because it is not about being quiet, per se. Our quiet style is the part of us that we know about, but are hesitant to explore. It is often the place where we find fun and creativity.

How Can You Tell?

How do we know which style to focus on? The nine aspects we talked about in each of the style chapters are a useful guide to help you isolate which is your interior style and which is the one you have adopted to accommodate exterior influences. Here are four blends to offer you a few examples.

1. The Giver and Wanter Blend: Looking for Love

If you identify with both the Giver and the Wanter and cannot determine which is yours, think about the way you look for love. The difference between the two styles is subtle, but telling. Givers yearn to be joined to another. You Givers want to be part of something or someone else. You want to be included.

Wanters, in contrast, long for others to join them. When you Wanters imagine finding your soul mates, you ride off into a sun that is setting on your own horizon. Here is something to ask yourself: When you long for connection, do you imagine being part of another person's life or do you imagine another person joining you in your life? If you imagine the person joining you in your life, do you then assume that you will receive the kind of love you really want?

When the Wanter Tries to Be a Giver, Love Loses

One of my clients reviewed the styles and determined she was a Giver. In fact, Renee gave generously to her friends and was always available when her parents needed her. She had helped one friend through a major illness and recovery, and though it was emotionally difficult, she found great pleasure in being a caregiver. She came to spiritual counseling because she longed for an intimate relationship, and knew she needed to identify and heal the issues that were keeping her from this. Renee said she wanted to find someone she could take care of with the same level of devotion that she had given to her friends and family. She told me that all of her past intimate relationships had lasted for a couple of years and then ended for various reasons.

I asked Renee to describe these relationships. As she did, I could see a significant pattern. Renee had also noticed the pattern, but had not known what to make of it. Her college boyfriend transferred from one university to another to be with her. Her next boyfriend moved across the country when Renee found her first job out of college. She was offered a new job, and another partner moved with her. Renee was in her early 40s when she came to see me, and as she told the stories, she counted about five men who had left their own jobs and homes and set up new lives to continue their relationships with her.

In terms of Renee's covenant, what is important is that she had a pattern of finding people who were willing to accommodate her needs. Renee was able to see this when we talked in depth about her short marriage. When she was in her 30s, she had a chance meeting with someone she had known in her childhood, and they both felt the sparks of romance. Before long, they fell head over heels in love. As she explained it, she did not want to leave her job, so he relocated from Denver to the East

Coast, found a temporary position in his field, and they were married.

About a year into their marriage, her husband found a permanent position about two hours from where they were living. He was willing to move someplace that would give them each an hour commute, but Renee insisted they move closer to his new job, vowing she would leave hers. After all, she told him, since he had moved the first time, it was only fair that she give up her job and make the move this time. She thought she would welcome the change.

She sincerely believed that she would do this. They went house hunting together, bought a house, and he moved in. Renee helped her husband with all the logistics of the move and supported him through the struggles of his new job during long phone conversations. She visited him every other weekend, bringing him home-cooked meals she had stayed up late the night before her trip to prepare. She wanted to take care of him, but she also kept finding reasons to stay at her job. Finally, after six months and many difficult discussions with her husband, Renee faced the fact that she was not going to move. Their marriage ended.

When Renee told me this story, I asked her if she understood why she chose not to move. She said she did not know it at the time, but now she realized that she never trusted that it would work out. She never felt that her husband really loved her, though he had made every attempt to convince her that he did.

I asked her to think about other aspects that may have influenced her. Was the relationship a good one? Did she enjoy her husband's company? He was a nice guy, Renee told me, but she really felt more satisfaction when she was engaged in projects at work than when she was simply hanging out with him. "The people at work understood me better," she said. "In all honesty, what I got from them felt more like love than what I got from him."

Renee's story is a classic case of an interior Wanter with an exterior giving style. Because she acted like a giving person, she believed the covenant she needed to heal was connected to serving others. Renee was nurturing to others, but her true style is that of a Wanter. Once she had to put herself on the line and trust that something would work out, she could not do it. She could not allow herself to be vulnerable. For Renee, the understanding she got in the workplace was a trusting form of love. Since it was connected to her accomplishments, she did not have to make herself vulnerable to feel it. Her husband's love was unconditional, and this was not something Renee was prepared to trust.

As we worked together, Renee realized that her covenant was much more tied to wanting recognition than it was to giving to others. She enjoyed giving, but she did not default to giving. She defaulted instead to all the aspects of being a Wanter: working for recognition, protecting herself from vulnerability, maintaining a safe distance. Renee also realized that if she continued to rely on her work relationships, which did not require her to be truly vulnerable, she would never have the intimate connection she wanted.

If Renee had continued to identify herself as a Giver and created a covenant that guided her to have more choice over her giving, she would not have touched the deeper issues in her life. Once she took responsibility for being a Wanter, she became aware of her fear of vulnerability and how it dominated her choices. This was her turning point, and it would have been missed if she had not taken the time to identify her interior style.

Renee had a quiet style as well, which she allowed herself to give expression to. She started journaling about her desire for a relationship, and ended up exploring the side of her that represents the creative, intuitive aspects of the Searcher.

For each of us, the quiet style is like a treasure waiting to be discovered. For Renee, to take the time to record and study her own dreams and thoughts was something that she did not fully allow herself to do as a Wanter. Once she found herself in the process of healing her covenant, however, she wanted to experience the strengths of all the styles so that she could integrate them into her life. Renee's treasure was the voice she found as she wrote her private thoughts—a departure from the work she did for recognition and the support she gave to others. This was just for her, and simply for the joy of creating.

2. The Searcher and Wanter Blend: Facing Anger

Another surefire way to determine our interior versus our exterior style is to observe the way we deal with anger. Givers will shut themselves down when they are angry. Wanters will find the emotion motivating, and Searchers will disappear. If your professional accomplishments and drive to succeed have convinced you that you are a Wanter, think about what you do in the face of anger. Do you find yourself getting involved in the situation, inspired to resolve the discord? Are you paralyzed, watching as others wrestle with the situation as you stand by, hoping for the best outcome? Or is the experience of anger so uncomfortable that you step out and wait for the bad feelings to blow over before you return?

The Searcher with a Wanter's Drive: Tony's Story

A friend of mine is a successful consultant, traveling internationally to offer expertise on manufacturing and productivity. He is a captivating speaker, and he charms his colleagues everywhere he goes. When I first talked to Tony about the styles, he believed he was a Wanter, as he has the vision and drive often associated with the style and could identify with the yearning for recognition.

Tony has been offered several full-time positions in his field that were more lucrative than his consulting practice. As we were discussing the styles, I asked Tony why he chose to be a consultant instead of accepting one of these positions. At first, Tony explained to me that he liked the challenge of responding to the variety of projects that his many clients provided. He said he looked forward to traveling and enjoyed the pace. He was not married, so traveling did not interfere with his family—in fact, he said, traveling kept him from feeling lonely. But he was torn, he conceded, because he knew he would have a hard time establishing a relationship—something Tony often told me he wanted—if he was not in a position to settle down.

Then Tony told me that the best thing about being a consultant was that he could "get out of the kitchen when he could not stand the heat." He said that if he accepted a position in a single firm, he knew he would be pulled into conflict—there is always conflict in any organization—and he wanted no part of that. As a consultant, he could exit as soon as the tension became uncomfortable.

Tony has created an admirable way of accommodating his intolerance for anger. He is successful, his life is interesting, and he has a simple and respectable way of sidestepping situations that he finds difficult. In one respect, this is to be commended. But another way of seeing this lifestyle is that Tony has devised his career around avoiding discomfort rather than facing it. He may also be sabotaging his chances of creating a healthy relationship. If he were willing to face the core of the pain he feels around anger and conflict, Tony would allow himself more choices and flexibility within his profession, which would probably increase the possibility of connecting with a partner.

Tony is a blend of a Searcher and a Wanter. He has learned to be motivated by recognition, and he has applied himself with the energy and the vision of a Wanter. But his interior style is the Searcher. He cannot commit to one thing, as doing so requires hanging in there and tolerating the difficulties. If Tony approached healing his covenant as if he were a Wanter, he would explore an inability to be vulnerable, since this is the Wanter's Promise Breaker. Tony would learn something, of course, but he would not confront and heal the spiritual agreement that is at the source of the Searcher's style.

If Tony claimed himself as a Searcher and then allowed himself to understand the way he acclimated to being a Wanter, he might also become curious about his quiet style. For Tony, this would be the Giver. Tony is not the first person who any of us would call if we needed help. He is kindhearted and certainly smart, but I have never seen him offer to help anyone. Those of you who are dominated by the giving style need to be mindful of your tendencies, of course, but all of us can benefit from giving when we do so in a conscious, responsible way. Serving others is a healthy thing; it feels good. No matter what our style is, giving can feed our hearts. I often wonder how Tony's life would blossom if he would allow himself to connect with the quiet treasure of generosity within him.

3. Interior Wanter, Exterior Giver: How We Define Success

Jenny is an example of a Wanter who has adopted a giving style to further her success. She is motivated, articulate, and at the beginning of her career. Right now, she is working as an administrative assistant, but she is applying to graduate schools to study environmental law. It is important to Jenny to stay at this job until she finishes her degree, as the salary is good and her employer is supportive of her future goals.

Jenny works for a boss who is more experienced than she is, but when it comes right down to it, he is not as bright. Jenny has talked to me about this at length. She has the quick wit to "show him up," but she has the focus and vision of a Wanter: She knows that to appear brighter than her boss would undermine the positive situation she has at her job, so she chooses to express the style of a Giver. She provides the administrative support the job requires. She is authentically kind and caring to her boss and to the others in the office.

Jenny enjoys the company of her co-workers, and she is somewhat satisfied by the tasks of her position. But isn't there something wrong with this picture? Is Jenny manipulative? Is it healthy for her to conform to the situation?

What's healthy is Jenny's awareness of her choice. There are certain things that most of us must do to get from one place to another, and often we need to be flexible and balanced in order to make our transitions as smoothly as possible. Jenny is not being manipulative. She is providing the skills required with full knowledge that she is capable of doing more, but she is not angry because she anticipates a challenging career in her future. She has taken responsibility to make this happen. She is using the strengths of her interior and exterior styles to create success. In fact, Jenny believes that when she graduates from law school and begins to practice, she will bring more to her job because of her experience as a Giver.

4. Interior Giver, Exterior Searcher: The Promise Breaker

I met Ann when her doctor referred her to me. She had been in a minor car accident and appeared to be confused and anxious about what happened. Her doctor determined there was nothing physical to address, so he suggested she seek counseling for stress.

As Ann and I talked, I recognized that she was an interior Giver and an exterior Searcher. She considered herself someone who liked to investigate different things. She was a housewife and mother, and she enjoyed nurturing her family and creating a home. She had also worked as a real estate agent for a few years, attended classes at a community college, and created oil paintings that she sold at craft shows. Now she was enrolled in massage school. When Searchers make these kinds of changes, they find the transition and novelty to be exhilarating. Ann, however, said she was hoping to eventually commit to one thing.

As a Giver, Ann's Promise Breaker was to speak up for what she needed: to use her own voice. The more we talked, the more evident it became that she was using searching as a way of not speaking up for what she really wanted. As long as she continued to dabble, she did not have to face her Promise Breaker. The searching exterior was a way of camouflaging her inability to stand up and use her voice.

A lightbulb went off for Ann when she and I discussed this. She realized that in fact she was angry with some of the dynamics in her marriage and that she needed to stand up and say something. Ann brought this issue to the counseling sessions in which she and her husband participated. The first time she spoke up for herself, she was very nervous. But as she continued to experiment with allowing her empowered voice into the sessions, she was able to gain comfort and familiarity. She created a faith-based covenant that says *When I speak up for my own needs as well as looking out for others, I will know what I want and will deepen my relationship with God.*

A Conscious Compromise

Jenny provides a strong example of making a conscious choice between the styles. If one of the reasons to determine your interior style is to better understand your covenant, another is that when you are not conscious about your blended styles, you live with the noise of their constant dialogue. Some of us are constantly torn.

Constantly torn—does that resonate with you? I find that as some of my clients find themselves relating to two styles, they become annoyed with the styles themselves, as if the descriptions could not be right. How could these people be two styles? In a way, it is easy to see. One of your styles is internal, created in response to your covenant. The other one is created to conform to external demands and expectations. When you are not conscious about choosing either one, you often find yourself in a battle between them. As one voice gently tells you to give and the other suggests that you be seen and understood for the great work you do, these styles can seem at odds, so you end up fighting within yourself.

Being conscious of the two styles is key. Sharon is an interior Giver. She is also a talented financial officer. Her job revolves around budgets and deadlines, and though she might prefer to spend her time with face-to-face contact, she directs her attention to spreadsheets and meeting the demands of her calendar. Sharon has a dream of retiring early and knows she must accomplish certain professional goals in order to do this, so she is focused on gaining the recognition she needs to earn the promotions that will enable her to meet this dream. She thought long and hard before entering this profession. She excelled in mathematics, but she knew that a career based on caregiving would feel more familiar. Her choice was mindful and deliberate.

Sharon is aware of her two styles. She knows she is a Giver, but she also enjoys her profession, even though it does not require her to be nurturing and giving. Because she is aware of her styles, she knows that the most comfortable thing for her is to default to caregiving. She also knows that by excelling in her job, she will manifest a certain dream. In order to do this, Sharon has chosen to limit her giving spirit in the workplace and to bring it more fully to her private life.

Sharon is also aware of the challenge her job presents in

terms of speaking up for herself—the Promise Breaker for any Giver—and tries to keep this in mind in the fast-paced and sometimes combative world of finance. It is not always easy for her, but she is aware of her choice. If her colleagues were presented with the styles, they would say that Sharon is a Wanter, but this is only because she exhibits some of the strengths of the style. The Promise Breaker of the Wanter—vulnerability—is not a challenge for Sharon, especially outside the workplace.

Many of my clients can relate to Sharon. They identify as Givers at home, but see themselves as Wanters in the workplace. If this sounds familiar, you may be one of many who have one impulse to be nurturing with your associates and another to be recognized in your profession. If nurturing is not rewarded in your workplace, you may have learned to quell this impulse, strengthening instead the skills you need to succeed.

This logic may seem to represent the simple reality that most things in life require compromise. But the truth is that true flexibility depends on your ability to be conscious of the decisions you make. If you are not aware of your choices, you can feel as if you were pushed or restricted. When you identify your interior style, you can recognize the choices that appear to be easy or familiar. The first reason to identify your interior style is to help guide you to your covenant, and the second reason is so that you can be conscious of which style you empower as you make your choices.

The Cost of an Unexplored Quiet Style

Jenny and Sharon were conscious of their interior and exterior styles, but neither of them was really in balance, as they did not have access to their quiet style. For each of them, the strengths of the Searcher—creativity, wanderlust, intuition—were not aspects they allowed themselves to enjoy. They were both healthy and their lives were satisfying, but allowing themselves to explore their quiet style would add the little something that could make the difference between a satisfying life and fully realizing the promise of the soul.

For some, the quiet style is the Wanter. The strengths of the Wanter include vision, drive, and boundless energy. Do you allow yourself these attributes? Or incorporating the generous spirit of the Giver might offer your heart tenderness and healing. And the free-thinking Searcher might be like a breath of fresh air to your life. When you create a faith-based covenant, you live in balance with all three styles. Until then, you may be missing out on an important part of your life.

Reclaiming the Dream:
David's Story

Some of you have an interior style that is totally camouflaged by your exterior style. You are dominated by the style that you forged in order to get along in the world, letting your interior style lie dormant until something awakens you to your covenant. When this happens, you may recognize a need to heal your spiritual agreement or you may want to reclaim it, as all covenants are positive when in balance.

This was David's situation. He was at a local hospital to consult on an architectural issue with the hospital administration, and after their meeting, one of them asked David to join her in attending one of my lectures. For David, this meeting was a life-changing event. I was describing how we each have a calling, and that healing our covenants allows us the freedom and flexibility to understand our calling. Some of us, I said, find that the calling is a way in which we can create and grow by serving others. This remark hit home for David. He experienced it as a moment of conversion, and there was no turning back.

David had trained to be an architect. A partner in a highly successful firm, he had worked hard to provide the benefits of an upper-middle-class lifestyle for his family. His two children were involved in sports and the arts, and his wife volunteered in community activities. To the outsider, David's life was humming along. But David had been feeling some uneasiness for a few years, he later told me, though he assumed that a little boredom now and then was just part of life. When he heard the lecture, he realized that he had left a dream of his behind. He recognized that it wasn't a bout of malaise he was dealing with— a bout that was bordering on years—it was his dissatisfaction in letting his vision atrophy. His conversion was to reclaim his dream.

David sought me out to explore what he had heard that day in my lecture. He was initially drawn to architecture, he explained, because he wanted to build facilities for the physically challenged that were warm, friendly, and lent a feeling of community through their design. When he was growing up, his grandparents lived in a nursing home that was just blocks from his house, so he and his sister often visited them on their way home from school, and his mother brought home-cooked meals to the nursing home several times a week. In many ways, David said, it was the best of both worlds. The family was close by, and his elderly grandparents had the nursing care they needed.

David also recalled the difficulties that his grandparents faced getting around the facility. They were both confined to wheelchairs, as were many of the residents. This was about 40 years ago, and despite the fact that the facility was built for people with limited mobility, there were obstacles to access everywhere. Most of the curbs did not have ramps, there were no handles in the bath, the cupboard handles were too high to reach, and the dining room tables were so low that the wheelchair arms banged into them instead of sliding underneath.

As a young boy, these obstacles struck David as easy to avoid, if only someone had thought ahead. He vowed to grow up and build a place that would be as welcoming to other aging residents as he wished this one had been to his grandparents. David was also a Giver, as he was well rewarded for the attention he gave to his grandparents and his family. But he was recognized for other strengths and talents as well, so his impulse to help others did not dominate his behavior. He enjoyed giving, but he was able to choose other behaviors equally.

When David started out as an architect, his children were young, so he joined a firm whose projects would ensure him a dependable income. The firm did not work on projects that reflected his vision, but he excelled at the work he took on, and his client base grew. He also found great satisfaction in the creative energy he had with his partners. Before long, David was pursuing new clients with projects from all over the world. He was always on the lookout for innovative ventures for the firm, and he found the globetrotting, fast-moving aspect of the job highly stimulating. In the blur of all the activity, his initial dream to build handicapped-accessible facilities receded into the background without his noticing.

When David came to me, he said he realized that his covenant was to experience God's love through serving others. Serving, he explained, was the ultimate act of being in tune with God. It gave him a sense of purpose and meaning, as it meant using his skills to open up possibilities for others. It also meant honoring the blessings he had received, because he was channeling what he considered to be gifts from the Creator. For David, architecture was an expression of reverence for beauty, form, and community. In its ultimate form, it was a way to work in concert with a God he considered to be a benevolent, loving spirit. It was clear to me as I listened to David that his covenant was already faith-based. He did not feel that he was commanded to serve others. There was no law-based agreement. For David, the challenge was to reclaim his faith-based covenant by living it.

David's interior style was the Giver, but his exterior style was the Searcher. He was always the one initiating new projects, and he often delegated the jobs to younger associates before they were completed. The buildings they were designing just didn't interest him, he told me. This suited his partners, as David's value appeared to be as much in creating new business as in his architectural skills, and his enthusiasm for new ideas was infectious to the young staff. David never connected his malaise with lack of interest in the architectural work, as he was also enamored with the busyness of the travel and the fresh challenges that came with new clients.

David had so conformed to his exterior style that he lost his ability to commit to the thing that was most important to him. His covenant—to serve others through his craft—was not included in his success. He now realized he had conformed to this role to distract himself from the fact that he had not pursued his original dream. That was where his sense of purpose was. In his moment of conversion, he realized that the buzz of activity in his life kept him from heeding his call. He decided to reclaim his covenant at the deepest level and follow the path of his dreams. When David left the lecture hall that day, he sped back to his office, brimming with the excitement of a child. He called his partners together and announced that from now on he would be working on projects devoted to physically handicapped facilities. They were hesitant, to say the least. David's idea, while commendable in their eyes, did not match the profit-making ventures on which his reputation was based.

After a few meetings over the next month or so, it became clear to David that his partners applauded his inspiration, but they did not want the business to invest in the kinds of accounts he wanted to work on. This is when the price of his covenant became clear. David understood their concerns, and decided to open his own office. He and his partners resolved the situation amicably.

As with all conversions, David's took an instant, and is now taking his lifetime. He has made a serious commitment to being in tune with his covenant. He has built a successful business by balancing his interior style as a Giver with the strengths he learned so well when he was living the searching style. When he longs for the buzz that his former lifestyle gave him, sometimes he answers the temptation and takes a quick trip or whatever it is that calls to him. But he finds that in the end nothing is as satisfying as just digging a little deeper into his new work.

Most importantly, David is conscious about creating this choice for himself. He now sees how he used his busyness as a way of masking his lack of purpose. He can differentiate between being on the move for the sake of motion and moving forward toward his goal.

EXERCISE 7

Understand Your Styles

It is time to return to the questions you explored at the beginning of the chapter. When we ended Chapter 4, you identified the style you thought might be your own. Try this again, but this time use the following phrases:

My interior style is _____.

My exterior style is _____.

My quiet style is _____.

Remember, the ultimate goal of changing covenants is to live in balance with all three styles. When you change your conditional law-based covenant to a faith-based spiritual agreement, you will not necessarily tone down your interior style or turn up the volume on your quiet style. Instead, no matter what your interior style is now, healing your covenant gives you equal access to all three styles. This is when you realize the promise of your soul, since you now have the freedom to choose your behaviors on a moment-by-moment basis as you go through your day, co-creating your life with God.

PART THREE

Changing Your Promise, Changing Your Life

CHAPTER 9

The Challenges of Changing Your Covenant

People are like stained glassed windows. They sparkle and
shine when the sun is out, but when the darkness sets in,
their true beauty is revealed only if there is a light from
within.

—*Elisabeth Kubler-Ross from* Quest: The Life of
Elisabeth Kubler-Ross

Change can be exhilarating. When we are in the throes of creating our faith-based covenants and envision how rich our lives
can be, it can feel like the first blush of love. We can imagine the
potential of living from our authentic selves.

Change can also be frightening. It is disconcerting to see the
world in a new way, no matter how ready we are. And once we

recognize how change might touch every facet of our lives, we may feel threatened, even if it is for the overall good. It also takes hard work. The initial glance at the positive outcomes of change holds great promise, but keeping it in focus can be a struggle. It takes effort, energy, and diligence.

The price of any kind of change is the experience of losing whatever we are familiar with. Denise, a colleague and friend who recently lost a great deal of weight, talked to me about the confusion and conflict she felt as a result of her change. As she journeyed through a year of exercising, personal growth, and healthy eating, she became more physically attractive. She looked as great as she felt.

The benefit of losing weight was everything Denise had hoped for. She felt more energetic, she liked what she saw in the mirror, and she was proud of having achieved a very difficult goal. But Denise also paid a price. There were aspects about being heavier that were familiar to her, and she missed them. Not only did she have to buy new clothes—that part she liked—but she also had to learn how to respond to a world that treats thin people differently from the way it does those who are overweight.

Men were more interested in her, which was something she had wanted, but now that it was a daily occurrence she felt a little uncertain. In the past, she had joked around with men, but if she began to flirt, they almost always backed off. Now, men initiated the flirtations. She knew how to deal with rejection, but how was she supposed to deal with desire? Women also included her in discussions more. Denise remembered many times when she felt as if other women had dismissed her based on her appearance. She used to shut down her feelings when she felt judged for her weight, and this kept her from becoming close to other women. Now, she was invited to be their friend.

In the past, she used to say that the bigger she was, the more invisible she became. Now, people noticed her all the time. She missed her anonymity and felt that she had to learn a new way of being in a social situation. Denise did not want to go back to being overweight, but she was surprised by how difficult it was to live with the consequences of her personal change.

"Many people say they are thin people stuck in a fat person's body," she told me. "I sometimes wish I could be a thin person back in my fat person's life."

The answer for Denise as it is for all of us who go through the kind of change that may be propelled by healing our covenant is to be aware of the possible changes and then take responsibility to integrate them into our lives. Denise's wish to be "a thin person in a fat person's life" was heartfelt, but what she really needed to learn was to be herself. For Denise, this entailed owning all the feelings of confusion, uncertainty, and unfamiliarity connected to making choices about how she wanted to be in her life now. She had made the choice to change; now she needed to make the choice to be. The goal was no longer a new Denise. Now, it was just Denise, and the challenge to be responsible for her experience.

When Covenants Come Between Friends

Many of my clients experience the same kind of ambivalence as Denise when they change their covenants, and often it is connected to relationships. The way people treat us is usually a reflection of how we treat ourselves. When we choose to create a new covenant, we will discover that some of the friends we made when we lived with our old covenant will no longer be part of our lives.

Remember my student in Chapter 2 who first told the class that he was meek, and being strong would feel "unforgivable"? This student, Phil, shared his personal journey with the class as he created his new covenant. The price of his change illustrated the ways in which our covenants—both old and new—influence all aspects of our lives.

Phil is a musician, a poet, and a gifted intellectual. He spent a decade pursuing his doctorate while supporting himself with research and teaching positions. Phil is a Giver. He helped others whenever they needed him, but what was more critical in terms of his need to change was his belief that being a caring person required him to be humble and meek—because, as the Bible says, this is the way "to inherit the Earth." In Phil's mind, to be powerful, or to demand that his voice be heard, was unthinkable. Phil was unable to make any choices for himself outside of these beliefs. In the long run, Phil's law-based covenant dominated his life to the extent that he almost ended his academic career.

Phil's Promise Breaker was to be strong, which in his mind meant appearing openly competent. Phil excelled in his field, but he refused to stand up as someone who was proficient and had the talent to be among the best. He watched as other students joined the graduate program and were awarded the honors and career opportunities he could have had. At the time, he looked down on their achievements. He saw the people who earned them as arrogant and said he was proud to be outside of their circle. He realized later that his resistance was based on his covenant, as professional recognition would betray his spiritual agreement to be docile and caring. In Phil's covenant, it was not possible to be both caring and competent. Then, after several years, his department demanded that he complete the doctoral program.

When Phil changed his covenant, the price for him was felt primarily in his relationships. Phil was forced to recognize that he had created a large system of friends who colluded with his covenant. When he blamed the "dysfunctional power trips" in his department for his own lack of progress on his dissertation, they agreed with him. They took his side when he reported on office conflicts, they helped him out of financial troubles, and they validated his rationale as each year passed and he missed his thesis deadlines. They did not challenge Phil to stand up and create whatever he needed to complete his degree.

He listened to his friends, offering sympathy and support whenever it was needed. People saw Phil as humble, gentle, and sensitive, which was very important to him. But as he began to explore his old covenant, Phil recognized that the people he chose as friends supported behaviors that did not ultimately serve him. Phil recognized that if he wanted to help others, downplaying his talents was not the way to do it. In fact, it was really a way of focusing more on himself than on service. Phil knew he was capable of excelling in his field, so he changed his covenant to *When I honor the gifts I have been given, I deepen my relationship with my Creative Force.*

Phil gathered his friends together when he was formulating his new covenant to ask for their support. Some of them applauded him, but some felt that he would no longer be a "sweet" guy, and they abandoned the friendship. Phil is still a sweet guy, of course, but now he brings his talents to the forefront. He has also created a new support system of people who encourage him to excel.

Three Levels of Price

We all pay a price, and it shows up in three areas of our lives:
1. Our relationship with ourselves
2. Our relationship with others
3. Our relationship with God, our Higher Power, or the Creative Force

Our Relationship with Ourselves

In Denise's mind, someone had to be wrong. Either the world made a mistake by treating her as desirable, or the beliefs she had about herself were not right. Denise now had to answer a question that often faces people who are in the midst of change: Would she rather be right or happy? She could stay with the familiar feelings of rejection—no matter what her body size—and be right about her internal beliefs, or she could let go of those beliefs entirely. She could make peace with the whole notion of being right or wrong, and create the choice to live with new, positive challenges.

All of us experience this kind of struggle as we change our covenant, and we each pay our own price for change: the experience of being on new territory, the risk of not knowing the terrain, the anxiety of following a path we believe is right but we have never traveled before. This is where we must trust our instincts, listen to new cues, and be mindful if the path circles back, asking us to retrace our steps—this is often part of the process. It's is not a simple task. We all face obstacles along the way. Eventually, Denise shifted her beliefs so that she could accept the possibility that she was a beautiful woman. Suffice it to say that our conversation has shifted from what was going on as she struggled with this change to all that is happening in her life as a result of her new beliefs.

Our Relationships with Others

A friend, Brook, told me a story about a graduation ceremony at the small elementary school she attended. The year was 1968, and many of the parents were distressed by a music teacher who wore his hair in a ponytail and parked his Volkswagen van in the school parking lot. When it came time to select the songs that the 50 students would sing at the graduation ceremony, there was much concern about what he would produce. But there was no need to worry. In a time of national discord—the graduation ceremony took place a week after Robert Kennedy was shot and a couple of months after the assassination of Martin Luther King

Jr.—they opened the evening with "Let Peace Begin with Me" and closed with "No Man Is an Island."

Brook has strong memories of rehearsing over and over again in the steamy auditorium and then singing with her classmates to an audience packed with the families of their shared childhood. They voiced the lyrics as if they were true, as if letting "peace begin with me" was a vision they could each hold for themselves, and as if "no man is an island" was really a call to work together. For Brook, there is still truth to the words. She finds herself humming them to herself now, more than 30 years later, especially "No man is an island, no man stands alone."

These lyrics hit home for me when I think about how our relationships change when we create faith-based covenants. I like to think of them in a more gender-free version—"No one is an island"—but the message is the same. None of us stands alone. Some of us may try to keep people at a distance, but very few of us want to live without the love and support of others. For some of us, our relationships are sometimes the very purpose of our being. In fact, we often set up relationships to help us maintain our beliefs about ourselves. When these beliefs change, our relationships feel the impact.

Many of you will find resistance from spouses, friends, or colleagues. And while some may discover that one price of a new covenant is the need to change or let go of certain relationships, others may find that the price is really the experience of accepting support. If your spiritual agreement keeps you moving, you may find that the price of being committed is the fear you feel of being tied down. Or if your new covenant requires you to be more vulnerable, your price may be the unfamiliarity of feeling your partner's affection. If this sounds like a dream come true, here is something to keep in mind: When it comes to change, having the dream is not the challenge. The challenge is accepting the realized dream.

Our Relationship with God, a Higher Power, or a Creative Force

Our spirituality is the reflection of our relationship with God or a Higher Power. When our relationship with God is rooted in judgment, our experience of the spirit is different than when it is based on co-creation.

There is something comforting about a conditional agreement with God. It's reliable. If we are Givers, we know that if we nurture others, we will be in good graces. If we are Wanters, we know that if we are never vulnerable, we will never risk "bad" feelings, and thus we will always be "good" in God's eyes. And as Searchers we know that we can count on our imaginative seeking to keep us in positive stead with the universe.

The Unknown Territory of the Spiritual Relationship

Once we let go of the agreement to win approval according to a law-based condition and adopt the idea of a deeper connection with God or our Higher Power, the dynamics change considerably. Now, we do not just have to default to a belief about what makes us worthy. Our covenant states that we are having an impact on our relationship with God with every choice we make.

This can feel risky, because it creates an unknown. For many of us, if we violate an agreement with a judgmental God, we expect to be punished. That is the deal. We may not like it, but at least we know where we stand. But when we make choices that deter us from our faith-based agreements, we are no longer breaking an agreement with God. Now, we are straying from a path that we co-create. We contribute 100 percent to this path, as does our Higher Power. When we wander from this path, we not only violate our relationship with God, we also violate ourselves.

We may suffer negative consequences, but these consequences are not in the form of a wrathful God. They are in the form of how we experience our lives. Because if our spirituality is a reflection of our relationship with God and if our new covenants deepen this relationship, breaking it weakens our spirituality. And the strength of spirituality is at the foundation of our lives.

The bottom line is that the faith-based covenant asks us all to take responsibility for our choices, and to live with the awareness that whatever consequences we create are our own doing. This is how we realize the promise of the soul. For many of us, living as if we could appoint God the master of our lives is much easier, as then we are absolved of accountability. But until we take responsibility for our lives, we may also be absolved of our true power.

The Challenges for Givers

Givers and the Self

If you are a Giver, the joy of serving others feeds your inner life, but it also keeps you from facing your unresolved issues around intimacy. You can depend on other people being in your life, as other people always seek your care. This is familiar and dependable. But when you stand up and ask for what you need, you risk the possibility of not being heard, or of your requests being ignored. If this happens, you fear you will be alone. For a Giver, being alone is frightening, since you base your identity on helping others. If you are not helping others, who are you?

This risk of not being heard and of feeling alone and without purpose is the price Givers pay for changing their covenants. If you stand up and say what you need, you will have to endure uncertainty. When you help others, there is almost a guarantee that you can lose yourself in their problems and never have to face your own. When you let others know that you have your own troubles, they may very well help you, but there is no guarantee. You must be able to rely on your inner strength, and if you are unsure about that part of yourself, change is difficult.

When you Givers take the risk to stand up for what you need, you often surprise yourselves. You may pay a price initially, but you may also discover a new, deeper part of your inner being that you had never explored, as you were always directing your attention to others. It is this deeper sense of self that will guide you to integrate your faith-based covenant and bring a sense of balance to your life.

Givers and Relationships

The price Givers pay in relationships is the fear of the unproven. You know that your generous spirits will keep your friends in your life, but what will happen if you create connections based on the value of who you are, not on how much you offer to someone?

What would change in your life? Would your expectations change not only in relationships, but also in work, in your creative life, and in your health?

Once you change your covenants and begin to stand up and ask for what you want, you may discover—and this can be extremely painful—that you have created a community of friends who are not, in fact, willing to love you for who you really are. You may discover that what they like about you is your capacity to give, not your need to receive.

If you are a Giver, when you heal your covenant you may have to end some friendships and develop new ones. And when you begin to form new relationships, you will have to take responsibility to be accepted for who you are. You will say what you need, and if these needs are not honored, you may make the decision to find your community elsewhere.

Givers and God, a Higher Power, or the Creative Force

If you are a Giver, imagine a life prayer that includes speaking up for your own needs. One of my clients, Annie, came to a halt in her process of changing her covenant when she took a look at including her own voice in her prayers. Annie had endured several losses, including the death of a child. She was able to talk about her grief, and could even allow herself to say she was furious at life, but when I asked if she was angry with God as well, she found the suggestion appalling. For Annie, to be angry with God bordered on blasphemy, as it does for many of us.

When we live with law-based agreements, voicing our feelings to God violates our promise. But when we live with faith-based agreements, sharing our real feelings with God strengthens our connection. As Annie and I worked together, she was able to include her emotions in her prayers, and she could trust that God would not punish her.

The Price for Wanters

Wanters and the Self

The price for Wanters is similar to that of Givers: When you change your covenant and become more vulnerable, you pay the price of acceptance. For Wanters, this means being accepted for who you are, over and above how well you perform at work, or because of your accomplishments. You Wanters believe that you are accepted because of what you do, not because of who you are. This is a way of keeping yourself free from the experience of vulnerability.

The Innocence of a Wanter

A client of mine, Olga, has worked long and hard to heal her covenant and balance her Wanter style with giving and searching. When she was in her early 20s, Olga was working in a start-up organization, and she was excited by the many possibilities she saw for improvement—and for her own recognition. When she described the situation, she said she had the "innocence of a Wanter," which she said meant that she truly believed that people cared about her only because she got so much work done.

Olga said she was often at her desk late into the evening, and admitted that as she worked, she imagined how impressed her co-workers would be with her accomplishments. Like a child, she looked forward to their approval and relished hearing their praise. Olga vividly remembered the morning when, as she sat in a meeting listing the number of things she had accomplished the night before, one of them leaned across the table toward her. The team worked together closely, so his question was delivered with tenderness and respect.

"Do you know you would be valued as part of the team even if you didn't get all of that done?" he asked.

Olga was taken aback—not because of her co-worker's honesty, but because she couldn't fathom the possibility.

"I would?" she answered, a baffled look on her face. "Why?"

Olga laughs about this now. She knows that her response had come from an authentic place, as it never occurred to her that she would be included, much less valued, simply for who she was. In fact, she says, when he went on to tell her that she was valued without having to do extra work, she felt uncomfortable. It felt too risky for her colleagues to care for her just for who she was. She now realizes that when she was recognized for her work, she felt as if she had some say over the situation. If she was liked for her achievements, she knew where she stood.

Being accepted for how much we accomplish does not require

the same degree of vulnerability and trust as being accepted for who we are, so this is an unfamiliar experience for Wanters. The experience of the unfamiliar is difficult for everyone, but it is especially intolerable for Wanters. You Wanters need to look as if you know what you are doing—this is connected to your drive for recognition, as you are afraid that if you appear incompetent, you will risk losing recognition—and this makes doing anything that is unfamiliar a real challenge.

One of the highest prices I paid when I changed my covenant was my experience of letting my guard down around others. My inner self was dependent on a carefully managed exterior. I had crafted a way of being in the world that I hoped was efficient, effective, jocular, and successful. These were all ways of creating an image that very few would try to peer through, so my inner self was protected. This was also the part of me I wanted people to love, of course, but it was hidden away. When I look back now, I see that I did this to keep myself safe from the possibility of pain. I can also see that I sometimes kept out love as well.

Once I chose to change my covenant and to allow myself to be more vulnerable, I had to trust that if others saw who I was underneath my achievements and strong personality, they would still accept me. The uncertainty, which was a high price for me, lasted for a long time. It still comes up, even today. But what also comes up is the proof that I am absolutely accepted when I am vulnerable, and now I can experience the pleasure of this acceptance.

Wanters and Relationships

The price you Wanters pay in terms of relationships is in taking responsibility for your own experience. Since this is new for you, you pay the price of uncertainty. And you not only struggle with accepting yourself, but you must also learn to reconcile with others. You have to own your role in the dynamic, learning to look at things in a whole new way. If you are involved with a Wanter, you have probably heard your partner imply that something is all your fault. Now imagine your partner saying, "I can see how I contribute to this situation." This is a big change for the Wanter.

Wanters and God, a Higher Power, or the Creative Force

The price for you Wanters in terms of spirituality is similar to the one you pay in relationships. Wanters tend to wait for a Higher Power to "prove" something. This is a way of protecting yourself. Once you allow yourself to be vulnerable, the experience of the Creative Force becomes available to you in ways you never imagined. When you develop a faith-based agreement and begin to live more genuinely with God, your spiritual life reflects this authenticity. You might become more inspired, more full of life, and more open to possibilities. These outcomes are all positive, but they are not the feelings you might be accustomed to having. No matter how good the outcome, when something is unfamiliar, you must be prepared to adjust to the change.

The Price for Searchers

Searchers and the Self

If you are a Searcher, the price of the unfamiliar is the effort of sticking to one thing. Sometimes when you develop a faith-based covenant that supports commitment, it may look as if the content of the commitment is where the difficulty resides. If it is a job, the work itself may seem problematic, but a lot of work is. If it is a relationship, your partner may bring all sorts of issues, but most people do. What is truly the price for you is the experience of sticking to one thing and the resulting feelings that emerge.

As with all styles, the price a Searcher pays is connected to childhood. Because you were not taught to focus your attention, the possibility of having to start now can feel daunting. Many of us take for granted the ability to follow through on something until completion. But commitment needs to be experienced at a young age in order to bring it into our lives in a healthy way.

Searchers and Relationships

Searchers have a wide range of interests and an energetic spirit, so you can be a lot of fun to be around. You will show up when your friends are in trouble, as you are sensitive to the needs of others. The companions that Searchers choose are often other Searchers. You share each other's journeys, and no one understands a Searcher better than another Searcher. There is no desire for commitment, no judgment, no need to explain when it is time to go. But when you change your covenant and create balance in your life with commitment, these friendships may be where you pay your price.

If you want to commit to a person or a job, you may discover that what your friends valued in you was your ability to get up and go at a moment's notice. You may no longer want to be tempted by this. And as you stay with your new covenant, you may need the support of people who can stand by you and listen as you work through the tenuous nature of change. Searchers will pop in to help a friend in a time of need, but being present day in and day out in a difficult time is not something you can provide. When you Searchers choose to commit, you pay the price of loss in some of your relationships.

Many Searchers I know have kept their old friends in their lives, but have created partnerships based on stability as well. As long as Searchers are mindful of their own commitments, I have seen this work out to be the best of both worlds.

Searchers and God, a Higher Power, or the Creative Force

Searchers are true spiritual seekers. You Searchers are always changing your relationship with God, so your spirituality is also in constant flux. Once you change your covenant and create a faith-based agreement that guides you to choose commitment to deepen your relationship with God, this all changes. You are not distracted by which direction is the right one. You will be focused on deepening one path. Once the distraction is gone, you must come face-to-face with whatever is inside of you that has kept you on the move. The discomfort of bearing witness to this pain instead of moving on is the spiritual price you pay.

When You Won't Pay the Price: Rose's Story

When we face taking responsibility for our lives, we may anticipate shouldering a huge burden. In actuality, we are liberated. But not everyone is willing to invest in the cost of change. Some get a glimpse of what it will take to live into their healthy covenants and opt for the familiarity of their old agreement. I do not encourage this, but I respect the decision.

Rose made this choice. She approached me after hearing me speak about covenants and the mind-body connection. She said she suffered from back pain and thought it might be connected to something in her life. She said she was ready to change.

Rose was from a strict Roman Catholic family, and when I asked her if she knew the prayer she awoke to each morning, she did not hesitate. She said she started every day by praying, *Oh*

Lord, please let me take care of those in need. When someone needed her, she explained, she felt she was closer to God.

The circumstances in Rose's life were difficult, so we worked with specific situations before exploring her covenant. She lived with her aging parents, operating as both a caregiver and a wage earner. Her father was an alcoholic. Her mother felt helpless and angry with her husband's drinking, and they fought often. Rose felt forced to mediate their disputes. Her brother, who also lived with them, openly used drugs in the house, but Rose was afraid of confronting him. She readily admitted that she was "carrying a lot," and linked the emotional weight in her life to the back pain.

In the beginning of our work together, Rose made great changes. She recognized that she had formed her life around the needs of her family. She acknowledged that they needed the care she was giving them, but also recognized that she did not have to be the only one providing it. When we talked about sharing the load, Rose asked her parish priest to help. He gathered church members together who had been through similar kinds of situations and they visited the home each week. Her parents responded well to the priest and the parishioners. Within a month's time, the priest had confronted her father about controlling his anger and his drinking. Her father began attending Alcoholics Anonymous meetings, her mother was attending Al-Anon meetings, and her brother had decided to seek counseling.

It was time for us to begin creating a new covenant for Rose, but I wanted her to be able to focus on the process before we began. In the weeks that followed the interventions with her parents, Rose continued to describe carrying the weight of the world on her back, so I asked her if there was something she wasn't telling me.

There was. Rose was in a secret romantic relationship with a priest—not the same one who had helped her family, I was relieved to hear—and of course she could tell no one. She knew he would not leave the church for her, but she felt unable to leave him. Now she described herself as being in a major bind, and acknowledged that this was probably the source of her back pain.

I asked Rose if she was getting what she needed from this relationship; she wasn't. I asked her if she was looking for other partners. "Yes, of course," she answered, but when I asked her what she was doing—for example, attending singles groups through the church, going to dances, asking her friends to connect her with single men—she said she wasn't doing anything. Then I asked if she was willing to leave the priest, and she said she couldn't. "He needs me," she explained.

Being a Giver, Rose's Promise Breaker was to speak up for what she needed. For Rose, this also meant turning away from somebody in need, because to do so would imply that she, too, had needs. The priest had not made any commitments to her, so she had nothing to count on, but she still stayed, because she felt that if he needed her, she had no choice. The notion of leaving him felt like death itself. For most of us, choosing to turn from someone in need is difficult—but the truth was the priest did not really need Rose.

The priest would carry on with his life and do just fine if Rose left him, but she would not allow herself to see that. In her mind, as long as someone needed her, she was in God's good graces. This meant she was unable to make any choice at all, since unless she cared for him, she would defy her spiritual agreement. A simple tweak to Rose's covenant would open the door for her. If she allowed her prayer to shift from *Let me serve others* to *Give me guidance as I choose how to serve*, she could consider taking responsibility for her own choices in service.

This was what she had done by asking for help with her family. She had chosen to serve them by asking for help, but she did not turn her back on them. In the case of the priest, however, she could not ask for help, as this would jeopardize their secret. His need for secrecy prevailed over her hope to heal.

I confronted Rose with the reality of the situation, pointing to the lack of real commitment on the part of the priest. She agreed with my observation, but refused to acknowledge that this could mean he did not need her. I encouraged Rose to talk about the impact of the relationship on her own life. She recognized how her old covenant was paralyzing her socially, emotionally, and even physically. She could see the folly of her relationship, but she could not leave it.

Knowing how much a part of her life her faith was, I then asked Rose if she believed it was God's will for her to stay with someone simply because he needed her. She said it was not God's will, but the power of it felt as if it might as well be.

This is at the core of an unhealthy covenant. When pressed on an issue, we will admit that God or a Higher Power is not governing our decisions, but we feel and we act as if God is in control. We feel and we act as if we have no choice, even if we know intellectually that we do. This is the power that our unhealthy covenants have over us. They are not divine will, but because they are promises we have made at this level, we behave as if they were.

Faith and Responsibility: The Fine Line

I know that the idea of covenants and God's will may trigger questions for some of you. For millions of people, "God's will be done" is the final decision. We leave it in God's hands or we let what goes around come around.

As a theologian, I have no doubts about the power of God's will. I have witnessed the positive outcome of faith in my own life and in the lives of others. Who knows how this works? There could very well be a God or a divine presence shepherding our fate. We do not know, so we believe, and this is what takes us on our spiritual journey.

When we are living with healthy covenants, our faith and our ability to make conscious decisions exist in harmony.

Ironically, the thing that would allow Rose to deepen her faith would be to take responsibility for her life and become the greatest woman she can be for the Creator. Right now, her inability to make a conscious choice is keeping her suspended in a place of dissatisfaction and resentment. She is not in touch with the miracle of her authentic self. Instead of experiencing the blessings that she knows God brings to the world, she experiences the burden that is inherent in a lawful covenant. But since it is a covenant, it feels as if it is outside her ability to change it. To Rose, the old covenant feels as powerful as the word of God.

Honoring the Loss

Letting go of old covenants is a form of loss, and experiencing this grief is vital to moving on. Grief is a part of any kind of change, even if the loss is a welcome one. We experience the same stages of grief when we lose our old covenants that we face in other deaths: denial, anger, bargaining, depression, and acceptance.

Is it worth the price? I can tell you now that my own experiences and those of the people with whom I have worked show me that it is. I paid the price of charting the unfamiliar waters of trust by learning to accept the love Ruth gave me. I took a risk that other Wanters will recognize is a big leap, and I committed in my own heart to accepting her love in the way it was given. In the past, my difficulty with being vulnerable meant I could not always feel her love, so I often thought she was holding back. When I changed my covenant, I had to pay the price of trusting that she—and others—were loving me enough. I had to recognize that the responsibility for feeling the love was in my hands. The uncertainty was a challenge, but once I made the shift, I felt as if I had emerged from a cocoon.

Change Is Within Our Grasp

Changing our covenants is about bringing healing and balance to our lives. When we are faced with change, no matter how healthy it is, it is always tempting to stay with what is familiar, even when it is uncomfortable to do so. It is simply easier to stay with what we know. When we do this, it may feel as if it is the will of God, or our predetermined fate, but the truth is that it is usually within our grasp. We may feel that covenants have the power of God, but in reality they have the power we give them. And we can use that power to heal.

CHAPTER 10

The Benefits
of Changing
Your Covenant

Days pass and the years vanish, and we walk sightless
among miracles,
Lord, fill our eyes with seeing and our minds with
knowing,
Let there be moments when Your Presence, like lightning,
Illumines the darkness in which we walk . . .
How filled with awe is this place, and we did not know it!

*Gates of Prayer—The New Union Prayer Book
for Weekday Sabbath and Festivals*

"How filled with awe is this place, and we did not know it!" This
is an experience many of us describe when we change our
covenants, as our authentic relationship to the Creative Force is

reflected in our everyday experience of spirituality. It is the promise of our fulfilled soul. We may live with a greater sense of ease and peace, or discover that feelings of grace and appreciation are more a part of our awareness. Our blessings may appear more bountiful than they had in the past, even if the reality of our circumstances is the same. Feeling more trust to turn to our Higher Power or devotional practice in times of need, and believing that when we do, our voice will be heard, will most likely be strengthened when we live with a faith-based covenant.

One way to talk about benefits is in terms of the balance and flexibility that permeates our lives when we integrate all of the styles seamlessly into the daily choices we make. Another benefit is the way this sense of balance and flexibility translates directly into our well-being.

Authentic Spirituality and Balance

When you change your covenant, it deepens your relationship with God or your Creative Force. You are able to make your life choices with the knowledge that being true to yourself deepens your connection to God. In turn, you are no longer dominated by one particular style. You now have access to all three styles—both their strengths and their challenges—which gives you the opportunity to live in balance.

How does strengthening your relationship to your Higher Power have an impact on your style? We all developed our dominant styles as mechanisms to keep us in line with our conditional covenants. When you change the covenant, you also eliminate the need to default to a particular style. You no longer need to be a Giver or a Wanter or a Searcher for the purpose of maintaining a secret agreement. The behaviors represented by all three styles are available to you.

Styles and Balance: Turning Promise Breakers into Virtues

When we create a faith-based covenant, we focus on our interior style. We celebrate its strengths, become aware of our Promise Breaker, and work to integrate them. As long as we are conscious of the choices we make, our interior styles are positive. By changing our covenants, we can live more fully into them while incorporating the other styles into our lives.

Your interior style is the one whose Promise Breaker is your key to healing. When you create a new covenant, you balance your interior style by exploring and accepting your Promise Breaker. If you are a Giver, you will learn to empower your own voice and have your needs heard, but not at the expense of your impulse to care for others. If you are a Wanter, you will get in touch with your vulnerability, but you will most likely remain as energetic and goal-oriented as always. And if you are a Searcher, you will allow yourself to commit, but you will not be forced—as many Searchers fear—to restrict your sense of imagination and creativity.

As we balance our lives, our Promise Breakers—choices we would never consider making—actually turn out to be virtues. We learn that the very things we believed would sabotage our relationship with God or a Higher Power are in fact great resources of power. They are often the areas of our lives that allow us to deepen the connection to our Creative Force, as they are the obstacles that in the past have kept us from our most authentic selves.

Three Styles, Three Virtues

Each style has a Promise Breaker and therefore a virtue all its own. If you are a Giver, your virtue is your own voice. If you are a Wanter, yours is vulnerability. And if you are a Searcher, it is commitment. All of us live more fully into our styles when we live with our virtues.

This can come as a real surprise. Before we heal our covenants, our Promise Breakers appear to be the last things we need to create healthy lives. Once we heal our covenants and are living with more awareness, we may be pleasantly shocked to discover that we are not undermined by these choices at all. In fact, the opposite is usually true. The virtue brings us discoveries and experiences that we never even considered having.

Givers and the Virtue of Voice

If you are a Giver and have not healed your covenant, chances are you imagine that claiming your voice—your Promise Breaker— would interfere with one of the desired outcomes of your style: acceptance. You Givers want acceptance, and you believe that the way to find it is to support and care for others. You may on some level believe that if you were to speak up for what you need, you would threaten the possibility of being accepted.

We are all creatures of habit, and yours is to downplay your own needs in the name of serving others. When you heal your covenant, you can change this. Once you are aware of how the covenant dominates your life, you then have the opportunity to make your choices outside of your old spiritual promise. When the choice is to behave in a way that feels like your Promise Breaker, you may be tempted, as Denise was, to stay with what you know (see Chapter 9). As Denise explained, when you make the choice to take the risk and find your voice, you may be surprised that it feels "like taking off blinders and seeing the whole picture."

When you find your voice in a conscious way, the experience shifts from a Promise Breaker to a virtue. Your impulse to give will be strengthened and more genuine. Finding your own voice will not keep you from helping others. In fact, it will usher in a new level of nurturing in which your support is more effective than ever. When you give through the lens of your old law-based covenant, you are not doing so as a fully empowered individual. Instead, you are giving because of your old agreement.

On an unconscious level, your impulse to help is really about winning the love or approval of your Higher Power. Once you heal that covenant and create a new faith-based agreement, you become aware of your decisions to give to others and to take care of yourself. You become aware of how choosing to support others *and* choosing to nurture your own needs will deepen the relationship to your Creative Force, as long as the choice is made mindfully. Now, when you choose to be a caregiver, you are doing so with the knowledge that your connection with God is not based on your willingness to support others.

Your new relationship with your Higher Power is based on the freedom to make either choice. This freedom is the virtue of finding your own voice. It brings an invigorating sense of energy to your giving, as it is now in your own hands.

Wanters and the Virtue of Vulnerability

The benefit for a Wanter is the balance of living with vulnerability. As someone who has lived with this dominant style, I can tell you that vulnerability does not at first appear to be a virtue for Wanters. We try to get recognition and understanding by working hard and achieving impressive goals. Vulnerability does not look like something that would support us in these efforts. In fact, vulnerability looks like the very thing that would undermine us. We fear that if we are vulnerable, we may appear to be weak, which would sabotage our mission.

I realized the virtue of vulnerability as I changed my covenant. Wanters want recognition and understanding because we believe that these things can provide us with the experience of love we yearn for. In fact, the way to experience love is to be open to it. We must allow ourselves to let the feelings of love touch our hearts. We must tolerate the confusion, powerlessness, joy, and risk of intimacy. We Wanters will usually avoid this, sometimes because of childhood experiences that convince us that it is not safe to trust, so we do not feel the love and connection we want, no matter how hard we work.

As I changed my covenant, I made the surprising discovery that when I allowed myself to be vulnerable, I felt the love and connection that I had expected my accomplishments to give me. Feeling love and acceptance no longer hinged on being acknowledged for my work. Instead, it depended on my willingness to be vulnerable and to experience my feelings. I discovered that in the past, when I did not feel the love I wanted, I assumed it was the fault of the people who were offering me their love. Somehow, they did not love me correctly, because if they did, I would feel loved.

When I allowed myself to balance my dominant style with the virtue of vulnerability, I realized two things. First, I was working hard to earn love by being recognized, while all the time what I really needed to do was allow myself to let love in. Second, the lack of love I felt was not because of what others were or were not doing; it was because I was not open to receive the feelings they offered. I needed to change.

Opening Up

Before I healed my covenant, my wife, Ruth, and I decided to see a marriage counselor to address some of the issues in our relationship. After a few sessions, the therapist gave us an assignment. He had observed that we were both committed to the idea of commitment itself. This idea occupied us so much that we were not able to commit to ourselves as well. We were so involved in maintaining the commitment that we had lost the purpose we each needed to feel as individuals. He told us that we reminded him of the nuns and priests with whom he works who are so devoted to a spiritual life that they cannot tell whether it is serving them.

Our assignment was for each of us to step back from the commitment we felt to the marriage and to determine, on our own, what was important to each of us as individuals. He told us to sit down with a journal and write about what we needed. "Not what you expect," he clarified, "but what you need."

As Wanters, asking for what we need invites us to take responsibility for ourselves in relationships. We avoid this task, because it requires us to be vulnerable. Asking for what we need exposes the fact that we actually have needs. We Wanters often find this difficult to face if we are not at peace with our vulnerability. The exercise forced me to realize that I had expected things from Ruth that I was not getting, but I had not been willing to take the responsibility to say what I needed.

When I healed my covenant, I was able to be vulnerable. I was able to say what I needed. I did not always get it, but being able to open myself up and ask was part of the benefit.

Searchers and the Virtue of Commitment

If you are a Searcher, the benefit when you heal your covenant is the virtue of commitment. When you are dominated by your style, you seek the freedom that appears to be found through constant change, and commitment feels like something that could suffocate you. You are simply not able to focus on one thing. You Searchers need to be free, but the thing that keeps you trapped is not the job, or the relationship, or the town you live in. What keeps you feeling like you have to move on is the agreement you made to God that keeps you in transition. No matter what you do to attain your freedom, you will not feel the sense of liberation you seek.

In fact, liberation is not what ultimately will satisfy you. Your journey is often devised, on an unconscious level, to help you manage issues that are not connected to freedom at all. Some of you are constantly moving in order to avoid your unresolved issues. Others are always changing because you do not have the skills to follow through on a project, or you cannot tolerate difficulty and decide to leave if things get tough. In all of these cases, you Searchers are on the move not for the experience of freedom as much as for the experience of escape. When you heal your covenant, you become conscious of the difference.

When you shift from a law-based covenant to a faith-based agreement, you begin to invite commitment into your life. The virtue of commitment is that it demands you to be present, to face your inner issues, and, ultimately, to be successful. When you experience success—whether in work, art, or a relationship—you are able to feel your true power. You are no longer carrying the burden you unconsciously believed you could shake if you just kept moving. Now, you will have the choice to stay in one place or to move. You will become sufficiently skilled to remain in one job or to accept another offer. You will not have to leave if a relationship gets tough, as you can hang in there through the difficult times. Or if you choose not to stay, you can break it off. Real freedom comes from choice, and without commitment, you Searchers have no choice.

The Benefit of Balancing Three Styles

The benefit of living with a faith-based covenant is the authentic relationship we have with our Creative Force. The support that is inherent in this kind of co-creating connection allows us to truly integrate our Promise Breaker into our lives, and in this process it shifts to being a virtue. We have more balance. At the same time, the strengths of the other styles come more easily to us.

The more we become conscious of our style, the more the distinctions among the styles fade away. We no longer have an interior, exterior, or quiet style. Instead, we are in balance with all three.

CHAPTER 11

From Disease to Ease

Learning that we can trust the creative energy of
Life itself enables us to relax more and more because
we know we don't have to make things happen by the
force of our will.

—*Swami Chetanananda*

The benefit of changing our covenants and creating a more authentic relationship with our Higher Power is experienced through greater balance and flexibility. As we discussed in the previous chapter, this sense of balance and flexibility is more readily available when we live with faith-based covenants. We have more choice over our decisions and can respond more genuinely, no matter what the situation.

Balance and flexibility may have an impact on our health as well. We will be able to manage our stressors in a new way, which can help to increase wellness. If we are faced with a serious illness, our authentic relationship with God will be a major resource, and the aspects of the different styles that we have integrated as our own will afford us the flexibility we need to heal.

To understand the ways in which healing our covenant is linked to our health, we need to revisit the holistic approach to healing that is inherent in viewing the body, mind, and spirit as a whole being. In holistic medicine, the word *disease* takes on new meaning. It suggests that illness may be a function of distancing ourselves from ease—*dis-ease*. This is more than a clever play on words. When we are at ease, we are in a better position to stay healthy. And if we do become sick, we are more prepared to respond to the trauma if we already have the tools that can help us manage.

The pivotal concept is *ease*. If illness is a matter of being separated from ease, then feeling a sense of ease can be equivalent to feeling healthy. In my work, I observe people experiencing a sense of ease when they heal their covenants. I see it when their new covenant allows them to bring balance and flexibility to their everyday experiences, and when they can choose how to respond to a situation in a way that reflects who they truly are, deep inside. The ease that changing covenants brings to their lives is in the form of overall well-being. It is a sense of health that includes the whole person—body, mind, and spirit—all in sync, all in balance.

I believe this ease is what we seek when we are on a spiritual journey. It is the comfort of knowing—and trusting that we are known by—our Higher Power or our Creative Force. It is the calm that settles over us during meditation. It is the protection we feel when we trust our Father or Mother, our God or our Goddess. This ease is the experience of sacred connection we gravitate toward on our journey. It is the peace that fills us when we sense our place in the world and the unity of which we are a vital part.

This is why a faith-based covenant brings us ease. When we change our covenants, we form a relationship with God or our Higher Power that is dynamic and alive. We become co-creators. We know that God's love is not conditional, as our faith-based agreements keep us connected to our Creative Force, no matter what we choose to do. This offers us a sense of spiritual security, as we are not earning God's love in fits and starts, depending on how well we keep our secret agreement. Instead, the love becomes a constant ebb and flow in our lives.

When we live with a faith-based agreement, we live in a way that honors our whole being as we deepen our relationship with God. This frees us from having to keep any part of ourselves cut off. We no longer invest our energies in maintaining a promise, managing a dominant style, or repressing our Promise Breakers. The sense of freedom contributes to our ease. We live in a way that is true to who we are and to the most positive vision of all we know we can be.

When we live outside of this truth, we carry an ever-present feeling of discomfort. Something inside us feels wrong. We are quickly rattled, succumb to stress, and react in ways we often regret. When we live outside of truth, we live without ease. This is, in a way, a form of *dis-ease*. When we heal our covenants, we choose our spiritual agreements through what is true for us. When we live every day in what is true for us, we live with a burden lifted. We are freed from the weight of false promises.

Changing Your Covenant, Managing Your Stress

Conventional wisdom tells us that lowering our experience of stress increases the possibility of strong physical health. I agree.

A high level of stress, as we all know, can leave us feeling run-down. When we are tired, our immune system is depleted, which means we catch more colds and flu and whatever else our bodies are too fatigued to fend off. In the old days, doctors ordered a "rest cure" for the sick. Now, more and more doctors are beginning to educate their patients about stress reduction as a form of health maintenance.

There are a variety of ways to reduce stress. Exercise and meditation are very effective. They can help us to flow with the kinds of external stressors in our lives over which we have no control such as traffic, workplace difficulties, and family situations. Stress reduction does not give us a way to control these external stressors, but it does help us manage the ways in which we react to them. I encourage everyone I work with to understand and manage his or her response to stress.

There is, however, a different way of looking at the idea of stress reduction. Managing the way we react to external stressors can get us through the day in a better frame of mind, but can't we do more? Does mitigating the impact of stress do us an ultimate disservice by masking the reasons we are stressed in the first place? What about the stressors themselves? What would happen if we could change them?

Though the wear and tear of living in a fast-paced, over-scheduled world is stressful, we sometimes forget that some of the most destructive stressors are not the ones we encounter on the highway or in the office. Stressors do not only exist outside of ourselves. The internal stressors we carry with us all the time can be as detrimental to our immune systems and health as those that occur in the course of the day. When our minds feed us negative messages, or when we constantly approach situations with fear or anxiety, these are internal stressors. They are often such a familiar part of our existence that we do not even know they are there. These stressors are rooted in a number of places: old family patterns, outdated belief systems, and like an umbrella that encompasses them all, the covenants we have made with God or our Higher Power.

Our faith-based covenants give us access to a wider range of behaviors and responses. This, in turn, allows us to feel more balanced, and we become more flexible in our day-to-day routines. Our responses are less rigid and we carry less tension. We no longer spend energy in an unconscious struggle to make sure that our spiritual promise is maintained no matter what.

Creating a faith-based covenant contributes to health not by managing stress, but by helping us to eliminate its source. When we heal our covenant, our responses to external circumstances are now rooted in a place of choice. We feel less turmoil when confronted with the stressors of daily life; in turn, our reactions are less stress-producing. When we intercept a stressor from a place of balance, we are more able to solve problems, find solutions, or just let them roll off of our shoulders.

Have you ever watched a dancer or a yoga student whose limber body allowed him or her to move in ways your body might find impossible? If you trained the way this person had, you might move with the same grace and ease. When we heal our covenants, it is as if our internal being takes on this kind of fluidity. We become spiritually supple, so we can bend and stretch in the face of life's changes with an ease that rivals a dancer's.

Covenants and Overcoming Illness

Another connection between a faith-based covenant and health is the increased flexibility we can bring to overcoming serious illness. When we are diagnosed with a life-threatening or chronic illness, we experience a life trauma. We are not only physically sick, but our lives are thrown into disarray, our relationships may be strained, and, depending on a number of factors, our finances could be at risk. For many people, a diagnosis turns the most basic assumptions about themselves topsy-turvy. Overcoming illness requires the flexibility to roll with the myriad changes that dominate our lives from the moment of diagnosis. This is where our covenant becomes imperative—in some cases, a life-or-death situation. Facing a health crisis is difficult enough, but if you already live in a state of rigidity, recovery is much more of a challenge than if you approach healing from a place of power and grace.

Faith-based covenants allow us to access all parts of our style as well as aspects of the other styles. They allow us to be flexible. In my work I have observed flexibility as the foundation of hope—just as I have seen rigidity as the cornerstone of despair—and overcoming a major crisis requires a vision of hope.

Faith and Healing

There is another way in which new faith-based covenants contribute to our health. Recent studies establish an undeniable link between a person's spiritual life and his or her health and well-being, as well as this person's ability to recover from illness. Research also demonstrates the efficacy of intercessory prayer, which many of us in the church learned long ago to take for granted, but rarely considered testing. Now it has been put to the test, and it passes.

Since this research reveals that spirituality plays a vital role in healing, it follows that we would be wise to engage in a form of spirituality that feels authentic and alive. When we heal our covenants, we deepen our relationship to our Higher Power simply by staying mindful of our new agreement. Our new relationship to our Creative Force may prove to make a critical difference when we need it most.

When Distant Healing Hits Home

Some of the research has been conducted by the Health and Healing Research Group (HHRG) of the Institute for Health and Healing at the California Pacific Medical Center. In 1998, a groundbreaking report issued by the HHRG was published in the *Western Journal of Medicine*. The report, "A Randomized Double-Blind Study of the Effect of Distant Healing in a Population with Advanced AIDS," was a culmination of a five-year effort that measured the impact of prayer. A close colleague of mine and the director of HHRG, Elisabeth Targ, M.D., headed the research.

For the purposes of the study, Dr. Targ defined *distant healing* as a "conscious, dedicated act of mentation attempting to benefit another person's physical and/or emotional well-being at a distance." When I originally talked to Dr. Targ about her study, I was reminded of the practice to "keep someone in your prayers," but Dr. Targ was careful to point out that in contemporary culture the intent of prayer can include practices such as energy healing or creative visualization.

A pilot study involving 20 patients and 20 healers and a second study with 40 patients and 40 healers were conducted. Patients with advanced AIDS (acquired immune deficiency syndrome) were divided into two groups that had been matched for illness, history, age, and T-cell count. One group received a 10-week healing treatment and the other did not; neither patients nor researchers knew which group was which. It is important to note that the usual criticisms of these kinds of studies is that healing may be influenced by a patient's belief in the treatment. In this study there was no correlation between symptoms or lack thereof and whether or not a patient believed they were in the treatment or control group.

The healers—all experienced practitioners—were located around the United States and Canada, and the patients—all with advanced AIDS—lived in the San Francisco Bay area. The patients did not know who the healers were, when the healing effort would occur, or which groups they were in. The healers represented many different spiritual traditions and averaged 17 years of experience. They volunteered their time. They were given a patient's photograph and first name and were told to "hold an intention for the patient's health and well-being" for 10 weeks, a total of about 60 hours of healing effort for each patient.

The results were surprising, even to me, and I already believed in the power of prayer. After six months, patients who received the distant healing showed a statistically significant number of fewer new and less severe illnesses, fewer visits to the doctor, fewer and shorter hospitalizations, and improved mood on psychological tests.

Dr. Targ followed up on the patients several months after the results were in, as she wanted to confirm that their knowledge of the study did not skew the results. She discovered that if a patient was convinced that he or she was being prayed for but in fact was not among those selected for intercessory prayer, that person did not experience the same benefits as those who were prayed for.

What Does It Feel Like to Be Prayed For?

Another colleague at the Institute for Health and Healing, Reverend Laurie Garrett, also works with healing and prayer, but from a different perspective. Reverend Garrett was a chaplain on our staff, and is aware of the ambivalence that some of her patients may have toward using prayer. She recognizes that this presents a challenge to using spirituality and prayer as tools for healing, so she invites people to explore their personal feelings about it. Reverend Garrett wrote about this process in *Ways of the*

Healer, a quarterly publication of the Institute. The article provides a valuable opportunity to understand our individual reactions to prayer and healing.

It is one thing to accept the scientific research that proves prayer can have a positive effect on healing, but when we imagine being in the role of the person who is the recipient of the prayers, our feelings may change. Reverend Garrett opens the piece by asking the readers to try a "spiritual experiment" and imagine what it might feel like to know they are being prayed for: "Just by invoking prayer, we are beginning a spiritual practice and encountering its challenges. Internal and external resistance is a challenge to prayer as a tool for healing. Entering into a spiritual way of knowing, being, relating, confronting, or trusting, is often not easy."

She then offers a prayer. Imagine that this prayer is truly being said for you. Explore what it feels like when your healing, your life, and your best wishes are the entire focus of Reverend Garrett's prayer:

> May the longings of your heart be in communication with the wisdom of your spirit, and the spirit of completeness, so that you may live with wellness, vitality, and peace; that you are empowered to laugh when happy, cry when sad, and practice compassion; that you receive love and support from a community of well-wishers, and that you give likewise with generosity; that you love yourself and love others, and that every day you find meaning, purpose and fulfillment. May music follow you and fill the beat of your heart with a rhythm that connects you to sacredness. Amen.

What was your experience of being prayed for? If you could imagine being sick or in need of support, how do you think you would feel about receiving this prayer?

The Power of Praying for Others

It's one thing to imagine being the recipient of another's prayer—but what does it feel like to believe that your prayers can touch the lives of others? Reverend Garrett suggests that we have more power to heal with prayer, but we limit this power. She calls it a "collective crisis of confidence": "This crisis of confidence is a form of denial about our power to effect change and to call on spirituality and prayer as tools for living, relating, and healing."

Reverend Garrett proposes that we simply may not know how to use prayer as a tool for healing, or that we feel insecure in general about how to pray:

> What should you say and how should you say it?
>
> Silently—out loud—a few seconds, hours or days without ceasing—dancing—shouting—singing—studying—whispering—with a musical instrument—intercessively or with petitions—thankfully with gratitude—with frustration and anger, fear and trembling, empathy and compassion.
>
> And how do you know when it has been effective? When can you stop? The key to doing any spiritual practice is practicing. Only through practice will you discover your truth, because spiritual practice is its own process of discernment. Trust yourself.

Covenants and Healing Prayer

When we change our covenants, we enter into an agreement in which all of our choices deepen our connection with God. We become more in tune with the impulses and impacts of our actions. This awareness brings us to a more mindful place overall, which in turn allows us to be more present and in touch with our lives. Our spirituality is a reflection of our connection with our Creative Force, and it is energized when we live with the connection in a conscious way.

This awareness can happen when we are willing to practice healing prayer, Reverend Garrett writes. We become transformed. This heightened connection with God can be one of the challenges of receiving and offering healing prayer:

Being transformed means living each moment with a spiritual willingness to be present to ourselves and others, being willing to accept or change ourselves and our community in thoughts and actions. This is my experience about spirituality. Too often we expect spiritual practice to be surrounded with soft colors, profound quiet, and the sincere whispering voices of people oddly dressed, or we expect spiritual practices to be guided by unmerciful rules, irrelevant dogma, or rigid tradition. We expect to sit back and enjoy the awesome, or sit down and endure the arrogant. However, spirituality need not be either of these extremes. Spirituality and prayer are eminently accessible. It does not require a fax, a modem, a phone, a pager, a building, shoes and socks, or even food or clothing.

You are always in the presence of spirituality and always able to access it. All you have to do is pay attention to the sacred part of yourself and create a context in which to express it. Right here, right where you are is your context for expressing your sacredness and honoring the sacredness of others, because here is where you are. Here is where you meet yourself and others and drop illusions and lies. Here is where you move forward and grow. Here is where you become whole and heal. Spirituality and prayer as tools for healing lead to a largeness in the moment—largeness of heart, awareness, connection, community, options, and perspective. Here is where you create the context for wrestling with the questions: Who am I? In what condition are my relationships? Who will I let into my life? Who or what do I sacrifice, and does that sacrifice contribute to my healing and the healing of others? What will I surrender?

Reverend Garrett acknowledges how difficult it is to embrace healing prayer. She used to facilitate the Spiritual Support Group for Women with Cancer at the Institute for Health and Healing, and says this has taught her that it takes a tremendous amount of courage and integrity to enter into spiritual practice in the midst of illness and disease. The Spiritual Support Group for Women with Cancer at the Institute uses a combination of prayer, meditation, guided imagery and visualization, movement, story-telling, stream of consciousness writing, creative art, therapeutic touch, singing, talking, supporting, offering options and information, and mutual sharing. Reverend Garrett explains, "I am constantly amazed at the courage and willingness of these women to face difficult spiritual questions. The power of revealing one-self, sharing oneself, entering into the vulnerability of spiritual practice and prayer is moving and wonderful, and awesome and terrible. It is the way of healing."

Prayers and Healing: What Does It Mean?

Research teams cannot provide an explanation of how prayer works, but it is worth noting that science does not necessarily require an explanation to demonstrate an effect. For years, for example, no one knew how morphine, quinine, or aspirin worked, yet they were known to be effective and were used extensively.

One treatment we now take for granted once kept an entire navy afloat before there was even language to describe how it interacted with the body. In 1753, when James Lind determined that lemons and limes cured scurvy aboard the HMS *Salisbury*, he could never have attributed it to ascorbic acid. In fact, the entire concept of nutrients was still generations away. But it appeared to work, and that was good enough. If the sailors could be treated effectively, the specific reason for the success did not matter.

The same could be said for prayer and healing. All we know right now is that long-distance healing also works. And since it does, it may prove to be an effective, low-cost addition to conventional medical care for seriously ill patients.

There are further NIH-funded (National Institutes of Health) studies underway at the Institute for Health and Healing. One is examining discreet factors such as frequency, distance, and dosage, which are part of distant healing, so that we can understand which of these, if any, is linked to efficacy. Another trains nurses and caregivers in intercessory prayer to see if they can influence outcomes with the same results as the healers who were used in earlier research.

Meaning Means Healing

The studies in intercessory prayer explore the potential of spirituality as a treatment. Research has also been conducted to evaluate the role it plays in creating an environment for healing. These studies speak to the need to heal our covenants. They demonstrate that when we are in touch with our spirituality, we are able to cope more successfully with illness and to recover faster. There are a plethora of studies that show this.

According to an article in the *American Journal of Psychiatry*, a study of 30 elderly women with hip fractures found that an ongoing belief in God and religion as a source of strength and comfort was directly correlated with a reduction in postoperative depression and the ability to move around after surgery.

Spiritual beliefs and practices of cardiac transplant candidates prior to transplantation were predictive of physical and mental health concerns at follow-up 12 months later, according to the *Journal of Religion and Health*. Of the 40 individuals studied, those who rated their religious beliefs as being highly influential in their life had better overall physical functioning, fewer worries regarding their health, and less difficulty adhering to the medical regimen than others. The study also found that those who prayed regularly for guidance in important decisions and who prayed frequently in private had an easier time following the medical regimen than others.

In a study of 232 patients undergoing elective heart surgery reported in the *Psychosomatic Medicine* journal, the death rate of patients six months after surgery was significantly lower for those who found strength and comfort from religious beliefs and practices. The social support of religious communities can be a factor in these kinds of studies, but in this case researchers found that even when social factors were controlled, patients who described themselves as religious were three times more likely to survive surgery than those who did not.

The *Journal of Holistic Nursing* reported on a study whose purpose was to "discover what spirituality means to patients recovering from an acute myocardial infarction and to identify the patient's perceptions of how spirituality influences recovery." It is interesting to note that the definition of spirituality used in the study was inclusive: "a life giving force nurtured by receiving presence of the divine, family, friends, health care providers, and creation."

"Spirituality influenced recovery," the study concluded, "by providing the participants with inner strength, comfort, peace, wellness, wholeness and enhanced coping."

When God Does Not Heal

As we heal our covenants, it is also important to remember that not every spiritual path will lead you on a healing journey. We may have a set of beliefs that will actually undermine our ability to heal.

According to the National Institute for Healthcare Research (NIHR), a nonprofit think tank that focuses on spirituality and health, research shows that certain types of religious beliefs can be harmful. These adverse forms of spiritual or religious beliefs include:

- Beliefs in a punitive God
- Beliefs that conflict with church or clergy
- Inflexible religious or spiritual beliefs
- Extrinsic religiousness

NIHR reports that extrinsic religiousness is perhaps the best studied of all the types of religious or spiritual beliefs that can adversely affect mental health. Extrinsically religious people are defined as those who "use religion as a source of personal gain or for mostly social reasons." These people may be the members of the congregation who want their names in big letters on a donors' plaque or who use the fellowship of the spiritual community for their own advantage.

Intrinsically religious people, in contrast, are defined by NIHR as those who "use religion to provide 'meaning' in their life and a framework for understanding all life."

According to NIHR, a number of studies have shown the following:

- Intrinsic religiousness tends to decrease one's level of anxiety on a daily basis.
- Extrinsic religiousness tends to increase one's everyday level of anxiety.

- People who've undergone a sudden religious conversion tend to be more prone to anxiety than those who become religious gradually over time.

This research points out the importance of understanding and healing our covenants, as by doing so we strengthen our intrinsic relationship with God. We need this kind of relationship in order to live more authentically with our spirituality, which may prove to be critical in the face of illness.

Over and above what the studies reveal, my own experience as a hospital chaplain has shown me there is no denying that spirituality plays a great role in healing. When you create your faith-based covenant, you can open the door to healing through your relationship with God or your Higher Power.

CHAPTER 12

Creating Your Own Covenant

Though no one can go back and make a brand new
start, anyone can start from now and make a brand
new ending.

—*Carl Bard*

We have taken a look at how our spiritual agreements can result
in defaulting to a specific behavior style. We have also examined
how our covenants have an impact on our health when viewed
in the context of mind–body–spirit healing. Now it is time to
identify our covenant and to create a new one.

Creating a new covenant realizes the promise of our soul. We
do this when we shift our connection with God or our Higher
Power from a conditional promise to a faith-based agreement,

as we align with our Creative Force in an empowering and co-creating relationship. This process is a key to reducing stress, living with an authentic sense of ease, and maintaining health. This chapter includes exercises to help you.

It is important to keep in mind that our old covenant is not necessarily negative or bad. More accurately, it allows one aspect of ourselves—giving, wanting, or searching—to dominate our whole being. When we decide to create a new covenant, we integrate the strength and virtues that may be a result of living with a law-based agreement and let go of the aspects of our style that no longer serve us.

If we are Givers, for example, we do not want to heal or change our inclination to give. We want to empower our generous spirits by allowing ourselves the choice over when we give and when we speak up for our own needs. The same holds true for Wanters and Searchers. We are not trying to eradicate the part of us that we have defaulted to in the past, but instead we will be working with God in a way that encourages us to make conscious choices, as doing so is at the foundation of our new relationship. And when we make conscious choices, we usually go in the direction of the more balanced, healthy aspects of all the styles.

My New Covenant

Like many people, I changed my covenant in the face of crisis. I was facing two losses: My mother had recently died, and Ruth and I were considering a separation. I felt as if I were losing the center of my very being.

I had been as good as I could possibly be. I worked hard, I played fair, and I did not intentionally hurt anyone, yet my life was falling apart before my eyes. My mind was clambering to make sense of what was going on. I knew I needed to still my thoughts and listen to my heart and my spirit, so I decided to attend a spiritual retreat to practice centering prayer.

For those of you who may not be familiar with *centering prayer*, it is similar to meditation in that it invites us to step back from our own beliefs and be open to the wisdom of God. Thomas Keating, who is the founder of the centering prayer movement, developed the practice as part of a series of retreats he offered as abbot of St. Joseph's Abbey in Spencer, Massachusetts. The retreats incorporated elements of both Christian and Eastern spiritual practice, and led to the development of centering prayer as a way to deepen one's relationship with God. In describing centering prayer, Keating says, "Jesus said, 'Watch and pray.' This is what we are doing in centering prayer. Watching is just enough activity to stay alert. Praying is opening to God."

When I bring myself to centering prayer, I sometimes bring an intention with me and then open up to whatever may come up. This is similar to meditation in terms of the extended periods of stillness that one enters. As those of you who have meditated know, the truth about sitting in silence is that it can be the noisiest place in the world, because this is when our inner chatter— our monkey mind, as Buddhists call it—will really let loose. When I went to this retreat, I kept my focus on the rhythm of my breath, watching thoughts come and go as my breath came in, flowed out, came in, flowed out. I wrestled with judgment, discovered old memories, felt my muscles tighten, and every once in a while, glimpsed a fleeting sensation of peace.

One afternoon I found myself seated in a garden at the retreat center. It was spring, and the dogwoods were in full bloom. My muscles relaxed and I felt open and receptive. I was thinking about the assignment that the therapist who Ruth and I were seeing had given to me, when we were each instructed to find what we needed for ourselves in our marriage. My thoughts drifted from the assignment to my memories about my mother, and then I heard my mother's voice.

"Do not be afraid," she told me. "Ask for what you need."

That was all I heard. It was that simple, yet when I went back to the meditation session that afternoon, I did just that—I asked myself what I needed. *I need to feel loved,* I thought. *I need to feel recognized. I need to feel valued. I need to feel . . .*

And then it came to me. This was my wake-up call. *I needed to feel.* I needed to feel the love and recognition that others were already giving to me. I did not need them to change; instead, I was the one who needed to change. That was how I could feel what I wanted. I got a wake-up call to be more human. I knew that being vulnerable meant I would face the feelings I had tried for so long to avoid: sadness, anger, failure, rejection, shame. But I also knew that vulnerability and openness were the only ways I could embrace the feelings I wanted: love, acceptance, validation, connection.

That's it? you may be thinking, That was so obvious! I know what you mean. I have witnessed the same kind of "Eureka!" with many of my clients. It is always a realization that seems simple, unless, of course, you are the person having it. When those of us who are Wanters realize that we are the ones who need to change, it's headline news. I work with people who constantly give to others, and when they finally realize they have a right to ask for what they need, the same thing happens—it is as if they have discovered gold. I also work with clients who have been searching for some kind of meaning in their lives, and when they realize that commitment itself will provide this, it is as if the weight of the world has been lifted from their shoulders.

My Faith-Based Covenant

I tracked my epiphany back to my covenant, *As long as I do not hurt anyone, I know You will love me,* and recognized that it was keeping me on a track of always having to prove how good I was. I knew I needed a covenant to honor my desire to work toward a vision, but also to support my need to be vulnerable. I wanted to depart from the idea of a conditional promise—*If I do "x," then God will love me*—and instead create a statement that said who I am capable of being, from my wisest, deepest self.

I now know God's love for me does not depend on whether I am a good boy. I know God supports me unconditionally in my quest to be a more full and loving person. I kept all of this in mind when I created my new covenant, and I came up with *I am free to be vulnerable as I work toward my goals and vision.*

Create a New Covenant

You are now ready to begin the process of creating your new faith-based covenant. Take out your journals again, as we are about to embark on another exercise to help you along the journey. There are no right or wrong ways to proceed, of course, because the faith-based covenant is not about right and wrong. It is about deepening our connection with God, our Higher Power, or our Creative Force.

This exercise will lead you through five steps, as follows:

1. Identify your style.

2. Examine your current life prayer.

3. Examine your Promise Breaker and your virtue.

4. Create your new life prayer.

5. Create your new faith-based covenant.

Step 1: Identify Your Style

Write down whether you are a Giver, a Wanter, or a Searcher. In order to feel clear with your choice, you might want to fill in the blank: "I know I am a _____, because when I am in crisis I _____."

Step 2: Examine Your Current Life Prayer

When you started working with your journal, you began with writing the prayer that comes to mind when you first greet the day. If you did not have one, you wrote what you imagined it could be. Take a look at the prayer and ask yourself the following questions:

- Does it emphasize one dimension over all others?
- Does it allow you the freedom to make a wide range of healthy choices?
- Does it give you the freedom to access your virtue?

Styles and the Life Prayer: Examples

When you live with conditional covenants, your life prayer is the request you make to fulfill your spiritual promises. Life prayers are linked to the covenant styles. Here are some examples of what the prayers might be for the Giver, the Wanter, and the Searcher:

- The law-based covenant for Givers is often *As long as I serve others, I know my Higher Power will love or protect me.* Therefore, the prayer is usually focused on asking for support in nurturing others. "Dear God," the prayer might say, "please help me to serve those in need."
- The covenant for Wanters might be *As long as I work hard, God will accept me or love me.* The prayer for the Wanter is often "Please help me to work hard and be strong."

- The Searcher's covenant is usually along the lines of *As long as I am pursuing new possibilities and change, I am safe with God.* The prayer for this covenant could be "Please help me as I search different paths."

These requests are good ones, but they are limited to the behavior that supports a law-based covenant. When you change to a faith-based covenant, your prayer will expand to include all aspects of your life. Some readers will find that their prayers already include the range of choice they need. If you feel that you can fully embrace your current prayer, do you actually bring it to life consciously?

Step 3: Examine Your Promise Breaker and Your Virtue

Your Promise Breaker is the key to living a life of balance. It represents a perfectly healthy part of yourself that you have come to believe is not acceptable. A colleague of mine has a couple of quotes taped to the wall near her computer. Though I have seen these words hundreds of times, I am still always struck by how they describe the process of understanding the Promise Breaker. The first is from Eleanor Roosevelt: "You must do the thing you think you cannot do."

Your Promise Breaker is the thing you think you cannot do. It is not what you *know* you cannot do—you are not entertaining actions that defy ethics, or the sound judgment of safety. It is what you think you cannot do, but can make the choice to do, if and when you are willing. And it is also the thing you must do, as this is actually your virtue. It is where you will discover your greatest strength.

Take some time now to write out your own Promise Breaker. If you cannot identify it, use the quote from Eleanor Roosevelt to help you out. Just fill in the blank: "If I must do the thing I think I cannot do, then I must _____."

Step 4: Create Your New Life Prayer

Once you understand your Promise Breaker, you are ready to develop a new life prayer. The other quote taped above my colleague's computer reads, "No problem can be solved by the same consciousness that created it," and is attributed to Albert Einstein.

This quote refers to the reasoning behind creating a new life prayer, which in turn will help you as you change your covenant. Your prayers as well as your meditations, your thoughts, and your dreams, all guide the way you run your life and make your choices. When you change your prayers and thoughts and dreams, you can have an impact on both the conscious and unconscious levels.

I find this quote especially helpful when I work with people who have invested a great deal of time and thought in personal and spiritual growth, yet still find themselves continually facing core issues. In my experience, this is because the very consciousness that created the core issues has not been addressed. Changing our prayers and the agreement we have with God can shift our consciousness. When we do this, the healing we are seeking is finally ours to choose.

Here are the steps for creating a new life prayer:

1. Take a look at the prayer you wrote in your journal when we began the exercises. Does it guide you toward a balanced life?

2. Next, take a look at your Promise Breaker—which is also your virtue. Is there a way you could weave this into your prayer to make it more inclusive and balanced?

Here are some examples of a new life prayer to give you a head start. Customize your own:

For the Giver

Guide me to remember my needs as I am in service to others.

Guide me to seek and to accept nurturing.

Guide me to find my own voice.

For the Wanter

Guide me to understand my responsibility in relationships.

Guide me to take risks and be vulnerable with others.

Guide me to trust.

For the Searcher

Guide me to commit to a path that enriches me.

Guide me to bring my creative energy to a grounded purpose.

Guide me to delve deeply into one area of focus.

Step 5: Create Your New Faith-Based Covenant

Before we begin this step, let's revisit the way you came to create your law-based covenant in the first place. As children, you made a secret agreement with God to help you make sense of your world. This became your covenant, and it helped you to survive and to grow, just as the law of God guided Abraham and his people. And, just as God's covenant with Abraham could not be contested, neither could yours. For the most part, it is an agreement of which you are not even aware.

God's promise to Abraham was conditional, just as our old covenants are. When you took out your journals and wrote your covenant by filling in *As long as I* _____, *then I know my Higher Power will* _____, you followed the same kind of conditional agreement that God made with Abraham.

Now, when you create your new covenant, it will shift from law-based to faith-based. It will also include all aspects of your style, so it will both honor the old and celebrate the new.

At this point, you have accepted your Promise Breaker as a virtue woven into your life prayer. Ironically, the life prayer—once developed to maintain your law-based agreement—will now, in its new form, become the final link that will connect you to your new covenant. Here are some examples of a new life prayer to illustrate this connection:

If You Are a Giver

If your new life prayer is "Guide me to remember my needs as I am in service to others," your faith-based covenant might be *When I consider my own needs and desires as I care for others, I deepen my relationship with my Higher Power.*

If your new life prayer is "Guide me to seek and to accept nurturing," your faith-based covenant might be *When I seek and accept nurturing as I care for others, I can feel closer to God.*

If your new life prayer is "Guide me to find my own voice," your faith-based covenant might be *When I speak up for myself and others in all relationships, I bring myself closer to my Creative Force.*

If You Are a Wanter

If your new life prayer is "Guide me to understand my responsibility in relationships," your faith-based covenant might be *When I take responsibility for my experience in relationships, I deepen my connection with God.*

If your new life prayer is, "Guide me to take risks in relationships and be vulnerable with others," your faith-based covenant might be *When I pursue my goals and am also willing to be vulnerable with others, I create a closer relationship with my Higher Power.*

If your new life prayer is "Guide me to trust," your faith-based covenant might be, *When I trust myself, trust other people, and trust God, I live in a more authentic relationship with my Creative Force.*

If You Are a Searcher

If your new life prayer is "Guide me to commit to a path that enriches me," your faith-based covenant might be *When I am committed to a path that enriches me, I am in a closer relationship with God.*

If your new life prayer is "Guide me to bring my creative energy to a grounded purpose," your faith-based covenant might be *When my creative energy is directed to a specific purpose, I am connected to my Higher Power.*

If your new life prayer is "Guide me to delve deeply into one area of focus," your faith-based covenant might be *When I am focused deeply on an area of life that is fulfilling, I live in peace with my Creative Force.*

Faith: Trust Your New Covenant

As you live with your covenant, it becomes an authentic part of yourself. It becomes who you are, which is essentially the promise of your soul.

You realize the possibility of living each day authentically. You are guided by your genuine beliefs as you co-create your life. There is great freedom, and there is also the challenge of faith. Faith does not just reside in God or any Higher Power. It is in each of us, and it is up to each of us to keep it alive.

I have a friend who used to be an aerial gymnast, traveling internationally with a company of circus performers. Karen is now a therapist, and we often discuss the challenge of creating new covenants. I believe her experience as an acrobat has given her great insight into the process.

When Karen talks about faith, she refers back to being under the Big Top. It is hard for me to believe now, as I've always known her as a professional who sits in an office, but when she was working for the circus she used to hang from the trapeze by her legs and then—*whoosh*—simply fly off, soaring through the air toward her partner, swinging on the other bar.

She says she would never watch for the person whose job it was to catch her. She had to believe he or she was there, steady-footed and prepared to grab her hands.

"If I checked to see if they were there," Karen explained to me, "that would change the timing, which would make it impossible for me to be caught. I simply had to have faith in them, and to believe they had my best intentions in mind."

Karen had faith, but she also took responsibility for the faith to work. "I would always extend my arms with a great reach, so I knew that they could catch me."

"It's ironic, but if I doubted *them*, I was doubting myself," she remembers. "And if I doubted myself, I could not extend my arms. It was not that they caught me that allowed me to keep the faith, it was that I reached out to them, believing they would."

Creating new covenants is our version of swinging through the Big Top. We take the same approach to faith that Karen describes. We do not take the risk of creating new covenants because we know God will catch us if we fall. Instead, we know that making the choice to create a new covenant is an agreement to live more deeply into our faith.

CHAPTER 13

Creating a Ceremony for Your New Covenant

Dance, my heart! Dance today with joy.

—Kabir

Your decision to create a faith-based covenant may take you on a journey that can be as challenging as it is empowering. Taking responsibility to become consciously aware of your style, facing your Promise Breaker, and then allowing it to be your virtue are all efforts that require energy, commitment, and a willingness to stay focused. Creating your new prayer and covenant is an undertaking that requires serious soul searching and careful thought. It is now time to celebrate yourself and your spiritual agreement with a ritual or ceremony.

The purpose of the ceremony is to honor you, the work you have just done, and the new relationship with God that is at the core of your new covenant. It gives you a place to express your joy and to share your pride in reaching your destination. A ceremony also provides a vehicle for you to ask for the support of your community as you live into your new covenant. You can use the ceremony to invite people to join you on your new path.

The ceremony can take any form you want—like your new covenant, it is yours to create. Some people ask one or two friends to join them, whereas others fill their home with a group of people and throw a party. I have heard about covenant ceremonies that were held on the beach, or set in a garden, or performed on a backyard deck. Some people like to have music at the ceremony; some prefer stillness. Whatever form your ceremony takes, I suggest you include the following steps:

1. Invoke the Spirit.
2. Let go of your law-based covenant.
3. State your faith-based covenant.
4. Invite community support.
5. Celebrate.

As you read about these steps and the different ways people use them, you will probably get some ideas for your own ceremony. Have your journal on hand to record your thoughts. Some of our best insights come when we are first introduced to something and our response is fresh. Put some time into the questions that follow each step and jot down all your thoughts as you read along. These notes may be enormously helpful once you are in the process of putting your ceremony together.

Step 1: Invoke the Spirit

All you need to do to receive guidance is ask for it and then listen.

—*Sanaya Roman,* Creating Monkey

Creating your new covenant begins with the change you made in your promise to God, your Higher Power, or your Creative Force. Now, instead of maintaining an unconscious and conditional law-based covenant, you live with a conscious agreement that deepens your relationship to your Creative Force. This is at the crux of your faith-based covenant. Because the new covenant redefines your relationship with God, the first step in honoring your promise is to invoke the Spirit.

If your ceremony takes place in your home, you can assemble your guests into one room as you begin the process. If you choose to have the ceremony outside, you may want people to come together in a circle, or to sit facing a lake, the sea, or the horizon in the distance. Invoking the spirit will set the tone no matter where you are. It shifts the mood from a gathering of friends to an acknowledgment of your new promise.

The most important thing about your invocation is that you create something that feels right for you. Feel free to take a moment and talk about what the invocation means to you before beginning, just to create an inclusive atmosphere for those who may not be familiar with it.

Here is a sampling of invocations you might want to consider. I include examples from a variety of traditions, and suggest a few different approaches you might want to consider as you think about the invocation.

Invocations and Style

One way to choose your invocation is to connect it to your style. Here are some suggestions that might work. The first one in each section is an example of an invocation I have written according to the needs of a particular ceremony. You may want to create your own as well. If not, feel free to use these examples as you like and to change any specific wording.

Givers

1. Stir up your power O Lord and come. Protect me by Your strength, save us from the dangers that may surround us and empower us to live life fully.

   > —*This prayer is by the author, Dennis Kenny*

2. I am bigger than anything that can happen to me, all these things, sorrow, misfortune, and suffering are outside my door. I am in the house and I have the key.

   > —*Charles Fletcher Lummis*

3. Queen of the Powers

   Bring me, bring out my own, my own.
   Let all that is needed be done well, be done well.
   Let me sing of your glory under the moon.
   I am ready for my personal power.
   I am the arm that does your work.
   I am the mind of your thoughts.
   I am the will of your achievements.
   I am the conductor of your power.
   I am the heart of your love.

   > —*Zsuzsanna E. Budapest,* The Grandmother of Time:
   > A Woman's Book of Celebrations, Spells, and Sacred
   > Objects for Every Month of the Year

Wanters

1. Almighty and ever living God, You hate nothing you have made and you truly forgive us.

   Create in me a new and honest heart that I may be vulnerable and trust you and those you have placed in my life.

   > —*This prayer is by the author, Dennis Kenny*

2. I will love you no matter what. I will love you if you are stupid, if you slip and fall on your face, if you do the wrong thing, if you make mistakes, if you behave like a human being—I will love you no matter.

—*Leo Buscaglia,* Born for Love

3. Dearest Goddess, I have come a long way this year, carrying my burdens. I would like to take them off my shoulders and give them back to you to recycle, to bury, to compost. Here, I offer you my resentments against friends, family, and (fill in your own specific concerns and thoughts here) and ask you to absorb them into your universe. Relieve me of them and allow me to walk more lightly.

—*Zsuzsanna E. Budapest,* The Grandmother of Time:
A Woman's Book of Celebrations, Spells, and Sacred
Objects for Every Month of the Year

Searchers

1. Almighty God, grant us the wisdom to see Your purpose, the openness to hear Your guidance, and the willingness to commit to a path You have provided for us.

—*This prayer is by the author, Dennis Kenny*

2. But where was I to start? The world is so vast, I shall start with the country I know best, my own. But my country is so very large. I had better start with my town. But my town, too, is large. I had best start with my street. No, my home. No, my family. Never mind, I shall start with myself.

—*Elie Wiesel*

3. Usually we regard loneliness as an enemy. Heartache is not something we choose to invite in. It's restless and preg-

nant and hot with the desire to escape and find something or someone to keep us company. When we can rest in the middle, we begin to have a nonthreatening relationship with loneliness, a relaxing and cooling loneliness that completely turns our usual fearful patterns upside down.

—*Pema Chodron,* When Things Fall Apart

Invoking the spirit establishes an atmosphere that supports you to let go of your old covenant, state your new one, and then ask your community for support. Once you feel the sense of connection you need to have with your Higher Power, it is time to continue with the next steps. Before we go on, take out your journals and answer the following questions:

- What is the tone that you want your invocation to set for your ceremony?
- What do you want your invocation to say about your process?
- What kind of invocation do you feel comfortable with? What would make you feel uncomfortable?

Step 2: Let Go of Your Law-Based Covenant

One doesn't discover new land without consenting

to lose sight of the shore.

—*Andre Gide,* The Counterfeiters

Letting go of parts of your law-based covenant is an important step in living fully into one that is faith-based. It is a way of raising the awareness of the impact of your old agreement and clearly acknowledging that you are choosing to live in a different way. When you let go, you are saying goodbye in two ways:

1. You are shifting the conditional law-based connection with God or your Higher Power.

2. The behaviors that were expressions of this covenant are now within your awareness, so you can choose whether to keep them. You will most likely choose to let some of them go. You will be saying goodbye to these behaviors as well as to your old agreement.

Planting New Seeds

A couple of my clients honored their old behaviors by creating rituals that signaled the transformation of unconscious behaviors into mindful choices. Eleanor, who I talked about in Chapter 6, wanted to weave a sense of gratefulness for her old covenant and behaviors into her ceremony. She was a Wanter who encountered repressed memories of childhood abuse when she experienced the grief of losing her father. For Eleanor, the decision to shield her vulnerability was truly based on survival. When she healed her covenant, she wanted to let go of her mistrust and caution, but she knew how difficult this would be. In a very real way, the behaviors she was letting go of had served her well. All of us are giving up familiar behaviors, but for Eleanor, they were more than familiar. These feelings were a lifeline. She thought that if she acknowledged this with strong intention, she might be able to move toward other behavior choices more successfully.

Eleanor held the ceremony in her backyard. It took place about a week after the last heavy rain of the winter, just as the change of seasons was charging the air. Eleanor had turned over the soil in her garden and constructed the furrows for planting that morning. I joined Eleanor and a few of her close friends as she asked us to gather around the plot, where the loam was dark and scented with the rich earthiness of spring. Eleanor asked us to cup our hands, and she dropped a small collection of seeds into our palms.

"The way this garden will grow represents the changes I am going to make," she explained. "The seeds are like my old behaviors, which I needed in order to grow into the person I can become. I had to be cautious and protect myself, and I am glad I learned how to do that."

At this point, Eleanor talked about how her childhood experiences forced her to protect herself. She thanked the forces within her that offered her this protection. She acknowledged how this armor, carried into her adult life, had limited her ability to connect with others. We all knew about Eleanor's process, but hearing it again was powerful. She talked about her heart, saying goodbye to the pain it carried, hoping the anger she had stored there could be put to rest as she lived with her new covenant. And then Eleanor asked her body to say goodbye to the suffering that it had endured. She thanked it for surviving. She said she would try to experience pleasure in her body now, as she had forbidden this in the past. We were all deeply moved by the courage and clarity of her words. I could feel her strength as she continued.

"Now it is time to move on," she said. "Like these seeds, I have a great deal of potential. But also like these seeds, my choices need to be transformed so I can come to my full potential."

Eleanor asked us to kneel down, sprinkle the seeds in the dirt, and cover them tenderly. She talked about letting go of her self-protection as we did this, asking God to allow the energy she had invested in protecting herself to act like the natural impulse of these seeds.

"I am letting go of the seeds of pain," she said, as we all knelt quietly, the cool dark soil sifting through our fingers, "and allowing each of them to transform into what they were meant to be: a beautiful, living flower."

As Eleanor continued the ceremony, we moved away from the garden, since she wanted to state her new covenant in a place that was separate from where she had invited the transformation of her old behaviors.

Her garden thrived, of course. A few months after the ceremony, Eleanor mailed each of us a photograph of her standing in the midst of the brilliant flowers, whose seeds we had all helped to plant.

I have only seen the use of a seed planting in the covenant ceremony one time, but there is one ritual I have seen a number of times. It involves writing your old covenant and behaviors on a piece of paper and tossing the paper into a contained fire. I have seen this done in a fireplace indoors and outdoors around a bonfire, and it is a powerful way to let go of behaviors and agreements. Most people speak about the covenant and how their style has dominated their choices as they witness the paper ignite and burn. As the ashes drift into the chimney or the sky, the process of saying goodbye is brought to a close, and the ceremony moves to the next step.

Take out your journals again and give some thought to the following:

- What are the issues, behaviors, patterns, or beliefs that you want to say goodbye to?
- How do you want to say goodbye?

Step 3: State Your Faith-Based Covenant

Taking a new step, uttering a new word is what people fear most.

—*Fyodor Dostoyevski*

When you begin to think about your ceremony, you may be the most nervous about this step. It requires you to face your community—which can be a couple of friends or a room full of supporters—and say out loud exactly what you have promised in order to create a more authentic relationship with God.

- If you are a Giver, you may say, *I now live with the awareness that when I include my own voice when I serve others, I deepen my relationship to my Higher Power.*

- As a Wanter, you might turn to your community and declare, *When I balance vulnerability with my vision and drive, I bring more truth to my connection with the Creative Force.*

- And those of you who are Searchers might stand up and state, *When I allow myself to be committed as I continue to seek, I live more genuinely with God.*

As you think about your ceremony and how you want to create the different steps, you may feel as if this step is going to be extremely difficult. Standing up and announcing your new agreement will engage your old relationship with your Promise Breaker and challenge your new virtues, no matter what style you are. If you are a Giver, declaring your faith-based covenant may feel impossible because you are voicing your own needs. If you are a Wanter, the possibility of making yourself vulnerable in front of other people may feel very uncomfortable. And if you are a Searcher, the commitment implied by making the declaration may be the most frightening thing you have ever tried to do.

This is why the step is so important. It invites you to be present and open with your deepest fears. And because it can be uncomfortable, you need to place this step in the center of the ceremony. You must not be distracted by your fears. The ceremony can include them and all of your emotions, but not at the expense of focusing on your new agreement. I placed this step in the middle of the ceremony, because the first two steps establish a sense of safety and acceptance, and the last two allow you to move beyond the experience of stating the faith-based covenant, inviting you to move into your community with it.

A Wanter's Courage

One of the most moving ceremonies I attended was offered by Jane, a client who worked on her covenant as one step in rebuilding her life after a profound loss. Jane is a Wanter who lost her husband to cancer when they were both in their 30s. When he was first diagnosed, she was unable to deal with the flood of emotions that she experienced. Jane was a partner in a law practice, and she was accustomed to being in control and getting things accomplished. All of a sudden, she found herself held hostage not only to her fear of loss, but to the complexities of the medical establishment. She felt powerless. When she came to see me about a year after her husband's death, she told me that one night when he was in the hospital she talked about her feeling of powerlessness with an oncology nurse. The nurse told her that there was something she could do. She could simply "be present" with her husband. The nurse told Jane that all he needed was to feel her love.

Jane listened to the nurse's words as if they were a set of instructions. She took a leave of absence from her law firm and stayed at her husband's side for the next few months. As she witnessed his decline, she remained a steady and compassionate companion, always remaining present and open to whatever was needed, just as the nurse had said. In the final days, Jane spoke softly to him about his life, their love, his dreams. She later told me that she was sitting with him when he died. His hand was in hers, and they were both facing the window, which looked out on an open, cloudless afternoon. She told me that she knew he had passed, but waited for a few minutes before she rang for the nurse. She wanted to watch the sky as his spirit left the room.

Jane told me she had looked forward to returning to work after the funeral. Once she walked into her office, however, she felt as if she no longer fit there. The speedy pace, the pile of documents marked "urgent," and her colleagues' interest in debating the intricacies of the law suddenly seemed irrelevant compared to what she had experienced. She told me that she had not realized it at the time, but she had become "soft."

During her husband's illness, many of the people in Jane's life told her they admired her strength. Jane knew they were talking about the courage it took to be at his side, but Jane later discovered that it was not the only brave thing she did. Being present with him as he battled the disease had required her to be vulnerable, and this was also courageous. It had opened her up to a side of herself that she had rarely allowed herself to feel, and one that she wanted to access more. She was confused, though, about which side of her was the "right" one.

As Jane and I worked together, she recognized that she was a Wanter, and that the vulnerability she experienced was actually her Promise Breaker. Once she put this into words, she could then choose to integrate both sides. She told me she decided to stay at her law practice, but with a decreased client load. This freed up her time so that she could do what many Wanters never take the risk to try: nothing. She decided to reserve a couple of empty days each week to see what she was drawn to. For a Wanter, doing nothing is an admirable step, as it requires a level of trust that things will simply work out, without any plan. She wanted to take a break from our counseling as well, and said she would get in touch with me when she was ready to create her ceremony.

Jane contacted me several months later. The empty days had been an intense and rich learning experience, she reported. Some were simply saturated with her grief. Others offered openings to new areas of her life. She bought a sketchbook and began to draw, she explored some of the local parks, and some days, she said, she just sat in her yard, "sinking into herself." It was some-thing she never would have valued in the past, as it was not productive, and she had nothing to show for it. Nothing, she said, but her peace of mind.

Jane held her ceremony at the beach. Ten of us joined her in a circle around a roaring bonfire. She invited the spirit, acknowledging the presence of her deceased husband. She said goodbye to some of her past struggles. She then stated her faith-based covenant—*When I weave my soft heart and my sharp mind together, I am at peace with my whole being and one with my Spirit*—and asked us to repeat it back to her. She stood silently as we did so. Then she said it again, but this time with a little more force, and again we repeated it back. We did this for about 15 minutes, answering her in kind every time. Sometimes Jane whispered, and we whispered back. Sometimes she shouted; sometimes she just said one or two of the words. She improvised with whatever came to her, which was why I was so deeply moved. As a Wanter, to allow herself to be in the flow—and to do so in front of others—took a lot of courage.

Jane and I talked about this at the celebration. She said she had been nervous about it. What if no one wanted to play along? What if it seemed too silly? But she wanted to go further than saying she was willing to be vulnerable. She wanted to actually be vulnerable as she said the new covenant, and this ritual allowed her to do that.

Take out your journals and think about your own covenant:

- How do you want to present it in your ceremony?
- What are your hopes and concerns for this step?

Step 4: Invite Community Support

Never doubt that a small group of thoughtful citizens can change the world. Indeed, it is the only thing that ever has.

—*Margaret Mead*

This step can be as challenging—and as liberating—as announcing your new covenant, as it also engages your Promise Breaker. If you are a Giver, asking for support can put you face-to-face with the fact that you, too, have needs and are now willing to state them. Wanters feel vulnerable in asking for help, and you Searchers are faced with accepting the commitment to your own word and to following through with others.

The step is challenging on another level as well. When you assemble your community, you need to feel that these people really want to support you. Because of your history of defaulting to a particular style, you may have established yourself with a group of friends who are not the best people to support you in your faith-based covenant. You may have to face the fact that your new agreement will usher in new friendships, which may be hard at first, especially when you approach this step.

The use of the term *community* can be a little misleading as you begin to think through your ceremony. It can sound as if you need to assemble a group of people, but that is not the case at all. The significance of the step is in the intention you make by reaching out, whether to a couple of friends or a group.

A Small Gathering

One of my clients, Esther, planned a small ceremony with two of her close friends and me. Esther's childhood was a difficult one. Her mother was physically abusive and constantly blamed Esther for causing problems. One of the messages Esther carried was that she was "always making trouble" for the family, which, according to her mother, was why she deserved to be punished. She also talked about how angry she had felt toward her mother, and the guilt she carried because of it.

I met Esther when she was hospitalized for a heart condition, and we continued to work together in spiritual counseling once she was released. During this process, she identified her original covenant: *As long as I don't make trouble, God will keep me safe.* The problem was that Esther happened to be an assertive, energetic person, so she often felt that she was making trouble. Esther was in a constant state of anxiety about whether her boisterous personality was breaking this agreement.

Esther never realized the double bind with which she lived until she explored her covenant. As soon as she expressed the outgoing side of her personality, she always felt tense and afraid, as if she were about to be punished. Now, she recognized that on an unconscious level she was breaking her covenant simply by being who she was. Once she came to this realization, she saw how deeply the double bind had affected her. She wanted to live in a way that allowed her to be free of it.

Esther wanted to surround herself with people with whom she felt she could be "more herself." She cautiously selected the guests for her ceremony. She only wanted to ask support of a community that she could trust would honor her desire to be free. Esther decided to invite two friends, and I was among them.

The ceremony was relaxed and casual. We met at her home. After sharing her invocation, Esther bid farewell to her old covenant and to the grip that memories of her mother had on her. She included us in this step, asking for recognition of how difficult her childhood had been. We acknowledged that the sense of anger she had harbored toward her mother was justified. Her mother's treatment of her was not acceptable, we assured her, and her anger was valid. Esther sat quietly as we told her this, taking it all in. I was moved by how intently she listened to us, as if she had been hungry for those words and never let herself open up enough to hear them in the past.

Esther then stated her new covenant: *When I fully express myself I am deepening my connection to my Higher Spirit.* She asked us for support. Esther invited us to remind her about her new promise if we saw her "shutting down," and we said we would. She asked us if she could turn to us for comfort when keeping her new covenant became difficult, and we pledged to be available to her. She asked us to share with her in the joys that self-expression can bring, and we, of course, said that we would be happy to. Esther closed the ceremony with a prayer of thanks, and we celebrated with simple refreshments. Later, she told me that once the ceremony was over, she carried a renewed sense of freedom and energy for days.

Here are some questions for your journal:

- Who will you invite to your ceremony?

- What kind of support will you ask for?

Step 5: Celebrate

Celebrate good times.

—Kool and the Gang

Celebrations come in many guises. I have been to covenant ceremonies that ended with dancing, or a drumming circle, or a lovely meal shared with good friends. The only thing that matters when you plan your celebration is to make sure that you create the environment in which you can relax, truly observe the work you have just done in your ceremony, and have a lot of fun. For some, this means taking a walk along the beach with a significant partner. For others, it means digging out the oldies and rocking the house until the wee hours. The celebration is important because it allows you to let off steam, releasing the tension you may have carried as you approached the ceremony, and it puts closure on the event so that you can start truly living into your new covenant and your more authentic relationship with God.

Invite a Guide

Over the years, I have discussed creating the covenant ceremony with a number of people, and I have participated in quite a few. I have seen ceremonies performed in a variety of places and in a wide array of forms, but there is one ingredient that has made the difference no matter where or how it was produced: the choice to invite someone to act as a guide. I strongly encourage you to do this. Guides can help you work out the details beforehand and can then preside over the ceremony, as it frees you up to experience your feelings and the support of the community. You can ask a friend, your therapist, your spiritual advisor, or an acquaintance whose skills you trust. No matter who it is, explore your hopes for the ceremony with this person. Your guide will carry out your directions, and if he or she knows what you want to achieve, this person may be able to bring more inspiration to the process. Guides can provide support in different ways, depending on your style.

Givers

If you are a Giver, you can use the experience of working with a guide to observe your feelings about claiming your own voice. I suggest you talk about your style with your guide to support you in speaking up about what you want. You may find yourself drawing a blank when you think about what you want in the ceremony, as you are so used to doing for others. You may want the guide to take the lead, but that would not be aligned with your new covenant. If your guide understands this, he or she can help you sort through the process while encouraging you to stay committed to your own empowered voice.

Wanters

Working closely with a guide is especially important if you have identified yourself as a Wanter, because it will be tempting to wear the management hat. You are accustomed to wearing it, and you are most likely competent at running events, but the ceremony is not about your competency. It is about your vulnerability and honoring your new connection to your Higher Power. If you choose to be the guide in your own ceremony, you may convince yourself that you are doing so because you enjoy it, which is probably true. But taking the role may also serve the function of protecting you from the vulnerability of simply participating in the ceremony and all the fears you have associated with it. Here is another way to think about it: If you were planning your wedding, would you want to be the officiator as well as the groom or bride? For Wanters, working with a guide beforehand and then stepping aside and trusting that the ceremony will unfold as it needs to is a rich exercise in ushering in your new covenant.

Searchers

A guide also plays a critical role for Searchers. Many Searchers have mentors who have played an important part in their lives, and this is a way to honor the individuals and the relationships. A guide can also help the Searcher with the issue of commitment. If you are a Searcher, the possibility of standing up in front of your friends and committing to a new covenant can be extremely uncomfortable. When you work with a guide, this person can support you before and during the event. You also get a dry run by creating your ceremony with a partner and committing to working with this person to develop the ceremony.

No matter what you have identified as your style, the process of working with a guide can provide you with an opportunity to rehearse the experience of standing up and stating your new covenant. This can make the actual event much easier. Rehearsing with the guide takes the edge off, which is important because it allows you to be more comfortable. But the real advantage is that once you feel more at home in your words, you are able to be more present with the experience and stand more grounded in your ceremony.

Singing, Dancing, and the Promise of Your Soul

Your ceremony signifies your decision to have an authentic relationship with God, your Higher Power, or your Creative Force. This is the foundation of living with the promise of your soul. In many ways, the ceremony reflects what Angeles Arrien described as "soul retrieval":

> Soul retrieval work is about singing, dancing, storytelling, and silence. Soul retrieval work is about knowing how to set sacred intention. It's about taking responsibility for your life in the ultimate way, which is "Will I live and lead a life that comes from guidance?" Or "Will I live a guidance that comes from the ego's agenda or the false-self system?" The true spiritual journey begins when you're more interested in living the authentic life that comes from taking action on guidance and aligning your personality needs with a deeper spiritual agenda.
>
> —*Angeles Arrien, from* The Four-Fold Way™: Walking the Paths of the Warrior, Teacher, Healer, and Visionary

When we create our new covenant, we live fully, aligning with a deeper spiritual agenda. When you get to the celebration step in your ceremony, it is time for the singing and dancing that make your soul come truly alive.

CHAPTER 14

The Blessing Moments

The closer you come to God, the more of you that has to die. The closer you come to God, the more of you there is to be born.

—*Tim Kellgren and Dennis Kenny, Lenten sermons, ELIM Lutheran Church, Petaluma, California*

As we deepen our relationship with God or our Higher Power and become closer, we learn to let go of the things that have to die, and discover new aspects within us, waiting to be born. We can do this because we now have the continual support of a covenant based on love and acceptance. We no longer live with a conditional promise, so we can shift our energy from keeping the agreement to living more deeply into it. This frees us to become more in touch with our choices, and to understand whether they support us.

Deepening Our Relationship

Any relationship based on freedom and support creates the possibility for growth and change, as we feel safe enough to turn away from the parts of us that may be familiar but no longer serve us. This is true whether the relationship is with an individual or our Creative Force. The knowledge of ongoing love allows us to take the risk to allow parts of ourselves to come to life. When we have a faith-based agreement, the choices we make deepen this relationship.

In some ways, living with our faith-based covenant can be a real challenge. It's one thing to say that deepening our relationship to God helps us to realize the promise of our soul, but is this really relevant to how we live, day to day? We want to balance the three styles, and to see the virtue in what was once our Promise Breaker. But, at the same time, it might be easy to let our faith-based covenants be buried under the weight of old habits and busy schedules. Is living with our new covenant going to turn out to be one more thing we have to do? In a word: *No.* The awareness we bring to our choices is at the foundation of living with our covenant, and this happens in the course of our day. We do not do anything extra. In fact, we can let the "extra" come to us, as long as we remain open.

Blessing Moments

We designed a ceremony in the previous chapter to signify and celebrate our decision to change our covenant. This is an important occasion, but it is just the first of the many, many times when we can step back and recognize the impact of our new promise. We will have the opportunity to see the influence of our faith-based agreement in action every day, in the little moments that make up our lives. I call these times our blessing moments. When we are aware of our blessing moments, they can help us to deepen our relationship with God. The relationship is always there, but the blessing moments help us to be present with it, as they remind us of authentic, conscious parts of ourselves that come alive when we are open to God.

Blessing moments come and go throughout the day, and many have touched me deeply. One such moment came during a conversation with a group of friends in a loosely knit support group. We all knew each other well, as we had been meeting for years. I was asserting a particular idea, but the person I was talking to was not responding in a way that I found convincing. I could see that he agreed with the point, but he was not acknowledging or recognizing me in the process. In his mind, why should he? I was in my full Wanter mode and kept pushing my idea, because in my mind, he had not understood me. Finally, my friend looked at me squarely in the eyes and said, "I agree with what you said. Are you working so hard because you also want me to tell you that you're okay?"

A lightbulb went off for me when I heard his question. I realized that this was not an isolated incident. I did want him to tell me I was okay. My need to push in this interaction was fueled by a desire to be recognized for having the good idea in the first place. In reality, I was not just trying to communicate the idea. I was trying to earn his acknowledgment of me for having it.

When I am open to blessing moments, I experience my vulnerability as the positive experience it can be, which brings me closer to my Creative Force. This realization was one of those moments. It required me to be vulnerable within myself and to accept the possibility that I had just been seen for my foibles, which, for a Wanter, is full of risk. I then took another risk and became vulnerable to the group. We discussed the interaction openly, and I felt their support in the process. I could bear witness to their caring. I could sit back, take in the lesson, and feel the nurturing they offered. I did not close down. I made the choice to be receptive as they offered their words.

This blessing moment occurred because I was able to hear that my friend's question was based in love. I made the choice to hear him as he intended me to and not as the protective, fearful part of my Wanter side might have heard him. It may seem like a small choice, but by making it I was then able to be open to the caring insights of my friends, and to integrate it as a deep learning experience. We are presented with these kinds of blessing moments throughout the day. They can touch us for an instant, and they can stay with us for our lives. Blessing moments remind us of the beauty of our world, the power of our hearts, and the authentic relationship we have with God. They allow us to live more consciously with our covenant.

The Big Moments

There are not only small miracles when we change our covenants, of course. There are also big ones. Once you heal your covenant, there may also be times when you create a big life change because of your new agreement. You might get to a fork in the road and be able to make a choice you could not have made in the past. Or you might face a part of your life that is not working and find that you now have the resources within yourself to take the necessary steps to improve it. Once you live in balance with a faith-based covenant, you may find yourself energized to make some major changes.

The big moment in my life, once I changed my covenant, was when Ruth and I were able to come back together after a separation of two years. Each of us used our time apart to live into our covenants. We each learned to balance the styles, and to recognize our Promise Breakers as virtues. Ruth is also a Wanter, so her faith-based covenant was centered on taking more responsibility for allowing herself to experience the connection she desired. Mine, as I have said, is grounded in becoming more vulnerable. As we each lived with our new covenants, cherishing the small moments and increasing our awareness of how these new spiritual agreements touched our lives, we found that we wanted to be together. We decided to start our lives as a couple once again.

This was a big moment. We chose to celebrate it with a recommitment ceremony much like the covenant ceremony, using the same five steps and the theme of acknowledging the old and ushering in the new. We invited family and friends, and asked Sheila, a religious sister, to preside over the ceremony. Sheila was intimate with the story of our marriage, separation, and reconciliation, and I found it enormously helpful to have her guidance. It allowed me to let go of managing the event and focus on the ceremony.

The day unfolded with a sense of graciousness and joy. We had put all the pieces together to create a ceremony about rejuvenation, empowerment, and the choice to live in a genuinely cooperative relationship with each other and with our Higher Power. The happy spirit of our recommitment emanated throughout the event. When it came time to say our new vows, Ruth and I stood together before our friends and family and said goodbye to our past struggles, acknowledging candidly the pain that we had each contributed and we had each overcome. Then we announced our recommitment to the marriage and prepared to read a piece of prose we had written for this moment. I faced Ruth, and we turned together toward our friends and family.

I saw my father lean forward as I began to speak, and watched my sons as they listened, though they had heard the words before. I saw friends from work, from the neighborhood, and from our church, all of them honoring our commitment of growth and change. I had been quite nervous before the ceremony, but as I read my parts of the prose I was filled not with the dread that I had anticipated, but with love, now palpable in the room. We shared a reading, parts of which follow:

> We have been through the flood and its water has born
>   us again.
> Overwhelming the water
> Pulling apart
> Pushing together
> The ebbs and flows
> The height and depth
> Its presence
> Through flood, fire and storm
> The water will bear us
> The flame will cleanse us
> The wind will form us and
> Love will always bless us.

Ruth and I then asked our family and friends to support us in our recommitment, which they agreed to do. And then the ceremony was over, and the celebration began.

I am certain that I could not have made the decision to recommit to my marriage if I had not made the choice to live into my new covenant. Deepening my relationship with the Creative Force allowed me, moment by moment and day by day, to take the risk and experience my true feelings. Living into our covenants is supported by the small blessings, which, in turn, make us available to the wise parts of ourselves that we need in order to make our larger choices.

I continue to make the choice to live into my covenant over

and over again, every day. This is true no matter how many times I recognize the small miracles, or how strong my relationship with God has become, or how often I can make the bigger choices from a more balanced place. I still need to remember to be aware of my style, my Promise Breaker, and my virtues. For example, saying vows in front of everyone at the recommitment ceremony was a real challenge. Not because I resisted the idea of recommitment—I found that to be both compelling and joyous. The hard part was standing up and saying it, as that made me vulnerable. As I look back on the nervousness I felt, I know it is something I still encounter when I am in a situation in which I feel vulnerable. My new covenant does not take that away. The thing that is different is that I choose to feel the vulnerability—usually—and to take responsibility for all the emotions that come with it. Now, though I still might want to hide in the face of certain feelings, I am aware of making the choice to feel them and be present with them.

You may find the same thing happening in your life as well. As you engage in the small miracles, the answers you may have been seeking to larger questions may become clear. As you make your moment-to-moment choices with the awareness of deepening your connection to your Higher Power, the more pressing decisions may not seem so overwhelming. As your life becomes grounded in the grace of the faith-based covenant, the big and the small can begin to meld together. In fact, you might find that the choices themselves begin to matter less once your spiritual experience becomes a guiding principle.

Realize the Promise of
Your Soul

I saw a bumper sticker a few years ago that said, "Having a great time. Wish I was here." It captured the irony of knowing, as we immerse ourselves in the distractions of daily living, that we are not present to enjoy our lives. When you realize the promise of your soul, you have the choice to be present to the fullness that your life has to offer in every blessing moment. You live in concert with your Higher Power, and can be at ease with all parts of yourself.

The promise of the soul is not about having a great time, of course, and co-creating your life with God does not mean the absence of pain. But, when life is difficult, you do not have to get caught up in what you did wrong, or in how you are being punished. Now you can turn to your spirituality and find the guidance you need. And once you find that guidance, you can make a number of choices to resolve whatever suffering or problems you may be facing, as now you live in balance with all aspects of yourself. This is the promise of your soul: to live fully, consciously, and in harmony with your Higher Power.

Now it is time for you to go out into the world and be willing to live fully with your faith-based covenant, knowing that every choice you make brings you closer to God. As you begin to live with your new promise, I leave you with a prayer: *May the small miracles in the world offer you blessings as you deepen your spirituality and realize the promise of your soul.*

Bibliography

Arrien, Angeles. *The Four-Fold Way™: Walking the Paths of the Warrior, Teacher, Healer, and Visionary*. San Francisco, CA: HarperCollins, 1993; 4–9.

Budapest, Zsuzsanna E. *The Grandmother of Time: A Woman's Book of Celebrations, Spells, and Sacred Objects for Every Month of the Year*. San Francisco: Harper San Francisco, 1989.

Buscaglia, Leo. *Born for Love*. Thorofare, NJ: Slack Inc. 1992.

Cameron, Julia. *The Artist's Way*. New York: Putnam Books, 1992.

Chodron, Pema. *When Things Fall Apart: Heart Advice for Difficult Times*. Boston: Shambhala Publications, Inc., 1997.

Gide, Andre. *The Counterfeiters*. New York: Modern Library, 1955.

Gill, Derek. *Quest: The Life of Elisabeth Kubler-Ross*. New York: Harper & Row, 1980.

Harris, R.C. et al. *Religion and Health*. 1995; 34 (1) 17–32.

Jung, C.G. *Psychological Types*. Princeton, NJ: Princeton University Press, 1974.

Keating, Thomas. *Open Heart, Open Minds: The Contemplative Dimension of the Gospel.* New York: HarperCollins, 1994.

Koening, H.G., Cohen, H.J., Blazer, D.G., et al. "Religious Coping and Depression in Elderly Hospitalized Medically Ill Men." *American Journal of Psychiatry.* 1992; 149: 1693–1700.

Kornfield, Jack. *A Path with Heart, A Guide through the Perils and Promise of Spiritual Life.* New York: Bantam Books, 1993.

National Institute for Health Care Research website: www.nihr.org

New Revised Standard Version Reference Bible. Grand Rapids, MI: Zondervan Corporation, 1990.

O'Donohue, John. *Eternal Echoes: Exploring Our Yearning to Belong.* New York: HarperCollins Publishers, Inc., 1999.

Oliver, Joan. *Contemplative Living.* New York: Dell Publishing, 2000.

Oman, Maggie. *Prayers for Healing.* Berkeley: Conari Press, 1997.

Oxman, T. E., Freeman, D.H., and Manheimer, E.D. "Lack of Participation or Religious Strength and Comfort as Risk Factors for Death after Cardiac Surgery in the Elderly." *Psychosomatic Medicine* 1995; 57: 5–15.

Rechtschaffen, Stephan. *Vitality and Wellness.* New York: Dell, 2000.

Riso, Don, and Hudsen, Russ. *1999 Wisdom of the Enneagram.* New York: Bantam Books, 1999.

Roman, Sanaya. *Creating Money.* Tiburon, CA: H.J. Kramer, 1988.

Roosevelt, Eleanor. *You Learn by Living.* Philadelphia: Westminister Press, 1960.

Sarley, Dinabandhu and Ila. *The Essentials of Yoga.* New York: Dell, 2000.

Sicher, Fred, Targ, Elizabeth, Moore, Dan, Smith, Helene. "A Randomized Double-Blind Study of the Effect of Distant Healing in a Population with Advanced AIDS." *Western Journal of Medicine*, 1998; 169: 356–363.

Tefilia, Shaarei, editor. *Gates of Prayer—The New Union Prayerbook for Weekday Sabbath and Festivals—The Pulpit Edition*. Central Conference of American Rabbis, 1975.

Walton, J. "Spirituality of Patients Recovering from an Acute Myocardial Infarction." *Journal of Holistic Medicine*, 1999; 17 (1): 34–35.

Williamson, Marianne. *A Return to Love: Reflections on the Principles of a Course in Miracles*. New York: HarperCollins Publishers, Inc., 1992.

Index